Fifty Divine Appointments

Gladys Joy! Bazemore

TEACH Services, Inc.
PUBLISHING
www.TEACHServices.com • (800) 367-1844

World rights reserved. This book or any portion thereof may not be copied or reproduced in any form or manner whatever, except as provided by law, without the written permission of the publisher, except by a reviewer who may quote brief passages in a review.

The author assumes full responsibility for the accuracy of all facts and quotations as cited in this book. The opinions expressed in this book are the author's personal views and interpretations, and do not necessarily reflect those of the publisher.

This book is provided with the understanding that the publisher is not engaged in giving spiritual, legal, medical, or other professional advice. If authoritative advice is needed, the reader should seek the counsel of a competent professional.

Copyright © 2021 Gladys Joy! Bazemore
Copyright © 2021 TEACH Services, Inc.
ISBN-13: 978-1-4796-1409-7 (Paperback)
ISBN-13: 978-1-4796-1410-3 (ePub)
Library of Congress Control Number: 2021911019

All Scripture quotations, unless otherwise indicated, are taken from the King James Version. Public domain. Emphasis supplied by the author.

A special thank you and recognition to—

Alvin A. Wilson

Daddy, Literature Evangelist, Pastor

You introduced me to colporteuring in real-life experiences while I was a child along with the companionship of angels and fellow colporteurs for which I will ever be grateful.

— Gladys Joy! Bazemore

Reviews

There is no greater feeling in life than to know that you were God's person, in God's place, in God's timing. In *Fifty Divine Appointments*, Gladys Joy Bazemore recounts providential experiences that will leave no doubt that she and her husband Larry were exactly where God wanted them to be. You will be blessed and encouraged by what God can do through people who are committed to Him. The exciting stories also remind us of the powerful place the printed page still has in reaching people for the Kingdom of God.

—Tim Leffew, Publishing Director, Georgia-Cumberland Conference

Fifty Divine Appointments is an outgrowth of several years of experience as front-line literature evangelists. Gladys Joy, along with her husband, Larry, have shared the gospel with countless numbers of people as they have conducted their ministry. Here, they share their experiences to inspire others for what God has done in their lives. As you read this book, you will be blessed to see the many lives that have been changed by the touch of the Holy Spirit through literature. May this inspire you to go out and do likewise. There is a vast need in every community for more Bazemores!

—Bill Beckworth, Retired Publishing Director, Southern Union Conference

When coming into contact with people that we would like to influence in a positive manner, one of the most important factors is that, by the power of the Holy Spirit, we must develop a familiarity that will allow people to be open to what we would like to share. In working with the author of *Fifty Divine Appointments* for several years, I have been impressed with her ability to allow the Holy Spirit to enable her to have the familiarity with people to inspire them. I have been impressed with her daily documenting of her experiences in ministry. This has enabled her to bring back these experiences with a freshness that will inspire the reader to experience these "Divine Appointments." These fresh testimonies are presented in a short story form that will inspire the reader.

—Michael Courey, Retired, Publishing Department Georgia Cumberland Conference

Having been associated with Literature Evangelism for 30 plus years I highly recommend this resource to all current Literature Evangelists, those considering Literature Evangelism as a profession, and to all others who may welcome a sense of joy and encouragement in their lives. *Fifty Divine Appointments* seeks to convey to the reader the providential and overarching grace of the Almighty at work in the lives of frail humanity, both in ministering and being ministered to, and the rich blessings that ensue.

—Bruce Germsheid, former Literature Evangelist and Associate Publishing Director

Table of Contents

A New Career 9
Part I LOAVES: BIG BOOKS & BIBLES 11
  1. The First Payment and the Last Payment 13
  2. Going Fishing in the Rain..15
  3. Chance Encounter?..17
  4. Water of Life for a Well Driller.....................................19
  5. No One Ever Told Her Before 21
  6. Seed Springing Up 24
  7. All the Right Answers 26
  8. She Said, He Said, and God Did That! 29
  9. No Washing Machine!...30
 10. Kelly—A Living Miracle 32
 11. From Disappointment to Divine Appointment.............35
 12. Not a Cold Card 37
 13. I Was Expecting You!..39
 14. He Shall Direct Thy Paths 41
 15. Golf Carts or Heat Waves..43
 16. From Office to Parking Lot 46
 17. Today I Was Praying and You Came!...........................48
 18. What Took You So Long?..51
 19. To Find Titus 53
 20. Recycling God's Precious Treasures 55
 21. A Real Investment...57
 22. The Trapper...59
 23. Spontaneous Joy!...61
 24. Three Divine Appointments..64
 25. The Sheep in the Bank 66

26. Thank You for All the Prayers 68
27. Already on Our List 70
28. Dog-Eared Books...72
29. Twice Adopted 74
30. In Spite of Opposition 76
31. These Dogs Bite! 79
32. The Wood Stove Order..81
33. Entertaining Angels 83
34. A Woman, a Dream, and a *"Happy D"*................................85
35. When We Meet Again..88

Part II SLICES & CRUMBS 90
1. The Value of Crumbs..91
2. Answers for Her Questions...93
3. Jump Out and Run!...95
4. Jason's Goals 97
5. Someone Special Behind the Door 99
6. Shocking News...101
7. Death Sentence Faith 103
8. A Little Angel, Beer Cans, or Vidalia Onions.......................105
9. Not Forgotten 107
10. A Dog, a Gun, a Prayer 110
11. Poking Holes in the Dark 112
12. Sudden Opportunity 114
13. For Melissa 115
14. Why Am I Knocking Here?..117
15. Mystery Lead Cards..119
16. A Call to Prayer...121

Part III A SIMPLE TOOL 122
Using the Character-Building Survey 123
Spontaneous Survey Responses 125
LE Character-Building Survey 128
Bibliography..130

A New Career

(Why I became a literature evangelist)

Hi! I'm Gladys Joy! I have a new career. I sell bread. You can order by the case, by the loaf, or by the slice. I give crumbs away for free. It's the Bread of Life that was sent down from heaven and delivered to us in a feedbox. Some of my best orders are taken around the dining tables in the homes I serve. I always ask God to bless this bread. I'm a literature evangelist!

As I came out of a time of tremendous grief and loss in my life, I felt God calling me to this work. I kept thinking about Jesus coming back soon, and I could not get His question out of my mind, "Where is your flock, your beautiful flock?" (Jer. 13:20, paraphrase). I began to pray, "Oh, God, give me a flock! Give *me* a flock for You!"

I got out my copy of *Colporteur Ministry*, given to me by my dad when I was age fifteen. I read it through and gazed at the two paintings called, "The Colporteur's Reward." In the first picture a colporteur is showing a book to a man who was raking leaves; in the second one, the man is gratefully shaking hands with the colporteur in heaven. I said to myself, "I want that! I want the colporteur's reward." I said it to God over and over, and He opened doors for me to come into this work.

He is building my flock and giving me precious glimpses of my reward now. Over and over my customers say, "I'm so glad you came!" It is the joy of my life to let God work out in me the answer to His question—to give me a flock and the reward of the joy that was set before Him beyond the agony of the cross.

Part I

LOAVES

LOAVES: BIG BOOKS & BIBLES

Please note: Names in the following stories have been changed to protect the identity of our clients.

Chapter 1

The First Payment and the Last Payment

It was midmorning. I found Bonnie and Martin both at home. He was all bandaged up from a terrible accident he was in the week before. He had two black eyes, and bandages covered his nose and the rest of his face, allowing just enough room to breathe through one nostril and leave his mouth free to eat and smoke. He sat there, telling me it was only because of the good Lord that he was still alive after being hit by a semi in the rear of his small trailer.

What a change from the first visit I had with them nearly a year and a half ago when I answered Bonnie's lead card for *The Bible Story*! She was all enthusiastic about getting the books for her grandchildren, and he was too busy puttering on his truck engine to come take a look. He had stayed busy just up until we got into price, then he came in and sat down, and immediately began telling Bonnie it was too much money. They had quite a go at it as she brought up reason after reason why she must have them for the grandkids, and how much they liked the books at the emergency room.

When they paused for a breath, I told Martin I was sorry he had missed the rest of the demo, but I was sure he could appreciate the books if I could just share a little with him. I grasped volume 7, which was open to Nicodemus and Jesus in the midnight visit. I told him quickly and simply the story of John 3:16. His attitude seemed to soften.

Suddenly he was on her side. He said, "I have more than this tied up in baseball cards."

She pointed to a case of expensive dolls and declared, "The bottom two rows of dolls would more than pay for these books!"

He relaxed and began telling her to put down a bigger down payment so her monthly would be smaller. It was amazing! As I wrote their order, he said, "You must have been doing this for a long time. You're a good salesman." I just smiled and offered to pray before I left with five referrals from his address book. He had told me he is the top sales manager at his company. That was the first payment.

Now I was dropping by to see them because for the first time they were a little behind on their payments and only had $20.48 to go to be paid out. I wondered if there was a problem bigger than Christmas recovery going on, and here he was, nearly killed in an accident! They were both glad to see me. She was happy to write a check and to be paid out, embarrassed to be behind, and just grateful her husband was alive.

They sat there and smoked until I could hardly breathe! As she handed me her last payment, I said, "May I ask you a question?"

"Of course," she responded.

> *"I thought you would like to know that you were the first people I ever showed the books to by myself. You were an answer to prayer when you ordered over a year ago!"*

"Have you ever wished you could stop smoking? If there was a way to do it that really works, without costing you an arm and a leg, that has helped thousands of others quit, would you be interested?"

"Oh, yes," she said. "I have been praying that there would be some way for me to quit. I tried the gum, but it makes me sick. And the doctors say if Martin could quit it would really help when they do his nose reconstruction." She eagerly took the stop smoking brochure.

Then I asked, "Would you like to know a secret?"

"Sure."

"I thought you would like to know that you were the first people I ever showed the books to by myself. You were an answer to prayer when you ordered over a year ago!"

They were thrilled. They signed up for our Bible course and said, "Come by any time!"

Chapter 2

Going Fishing in the Rain

Question: Do fish bite better on a rainy day? **Answer**: Only if I'm fishing!

The day was drizzly, cold, and miserable, so I prayed for wisdom and claimed God's promise of 1,000 ways to provide for me of which I know nothing.

My first lead was not home, but I was in a nice subdivision, so I prayed, "Father, in all these houses there must be someone home who will say yes and look at the books. Please give me the grit to go on!" Then I started in. There were some polite refusals, and some took the flyers saying they'd look it over. I worked my way into the cul-de-sac that was farthest back in the neighborhood. I prayed again and again, "Father, please give me someone in this neighborhood."

I knocked at one more door. A man and his teenage daughter opened it, saying, "Come in out of the rain!"

He introduced himself as Dan, and his wife Pam joined us a moment later. Small children were playing, and a baby stood in a playpen. When I asked how many children they had, he said, "Eight still at home. We've been in foster care for six years now. It keeps the house full."

Pam said, "The kids always grab *The Bible Story* first when we go to the doctor's office. They love that book. I'm sorry we can't look right now. We're leaving for a doctor's appointment for Dan's eyes. They were badly burned last week at work. See!" She lifted his glasses so I could see how red they were.

"Chemical burn," he added. "So, I'm home recovering my sight. Could you come back at 4:00 p.m.?"

At 4:00 p.m. Dan was there with all the kids gathered around to see the books. Pam was out on errands. After just a little time in volume 1,

Dan said, "Do you have those Bible stories for adults too? I saw them in the flyer."

I replied, "Yes, I'll be glad to share that with you in a moment."

He said, "I think they would really help me. I preach and teach Sunday school a lot. How much are they?"

I said, "That's a good question. Let me share a little more about *The Bible Story*, then I'll show you the *Bible Reference Library*, and then I'll answer that question, OK?"

I put out *The Bible Story* cover spread, and the kids crowded around. The teenage daughter, Lisa, sat on the arm of the couch next to her dad. They were intensely focused on the books. In a few minutes kids with books were all around.

Dan told me they had already adopted four of the children. Their only biological child is grown and married. As he mentioned trying to adopt more of the kids, Lisa smiled widely and said, "I'm already adopted!" Then she sat there, helping to sell the books to him. "They'll be such a big help in your church work, Daddy!" she said.

As Dan made his order he asked, "How did you get my name?"

I said, "I prayed about where I should go in the rain, and God kept you home today for your eyes."

I felt Jesus was keeping His promise: "I will make you fishers of men" (Matt. 4:19). What a joy to go fishing—even in the rain!

Chapter 3

Chance Encounter?

The country road stretched before me as I scanned mailboxes for number 5704. A few numbers flashed by, and I realized I'd have a long way to go to find this one. My brain tuned in to watch for toys and minivans, and soon I was in the driveway of a home with the right stuff.

As I walked toward the house with my case and *The Bible Story* flyers, the lady of the house, Melody, came through the carport in her bathing suit. She greeted me warmly, saying she was just out back getting a suntan. She said she would invite me in, but the house was a mess and her three-year-old was asleep.

I canvassed her briefly right there. She liked *The Bible Story*. She remarked, "Isn't it strange? I was just thinking I needed something like this on my way home from Sunday school this week!" She couldn't get into a big order right then, so I offered her my paperback of *The Bible Story* and *Bible Readings*. She gladly purchased them and signed up for the Bible course.

She said, "Business at our family restaurant is picking up for the summer. Please call me in June, and I'll get my sister to come look at these books too."

The next week we had that appointment. Again, Melody was happy to see me. Her two youngsters joined us at the dining room table. A big rainstorm was starting, so her sister did not show up. As I showed them the books, her son ran and got their little sample of *The Bible Story* book, and Melody told me how she was enjoying the Bible lessons through the mail.

When I began explaining the indexes in volume 10, Melody got really excited. She took the book from me and scanned the "Complete List of the 411 Stories." She exclaimed, "Oh, this would be worth the whole set! Here's a complete outline of the Bible!

I know Bible stories, but I never know where to find them in my Bible. This is wonderful!"

She was excited about *Bible Readings* because it matched the little one she was already using, and she was delighted when I showed her the *Vibrant Life* magazine. As she contemplated which payment plan to use, she told me that their little restaurant, which seats fifty at a time, is now serving 250 customers per night—catfish, steak, etc. And her little boy began naming off menu items.

Finally, Melody decided, "I'll just put it on my Visa and take care of it that way." As we finished the paperwork, she said, "Thank you so much for remembering to call me back!"

Was it just a chance encounter that I met Melody? I don't think so!

Chapter 4

Water of Life for a Well Driller

Christmas decorations and lights caught my attention along with children's toys and a trampoline in the yard of this country home. I pulled off the dirt road into a driveway crowded by a load of well-drilling supplies. After running several leads with no success, I hoped someone would be willing to talk to Bruce—my supervisor—and me about *The Bible Story* library. A man in construction work clothes seemed to be directing the others. I asked if his wife was inside. He waved me to the back porch saying, "Yes, she'll talk to you."

I went inside with my little questionnaire clipboard while Bruce moved my vehicle out of the way of the well drillers. Molly was ready to talk with me about spiritual things. She had strong opinions about how important religious training is for children and where the most important place is for them to learn about the Bible. She was ready to look at *The Bible Story* set. So, I went out for my case.

Her husband Horace along with Bruce came back inside with me. Horace called out, "Honey, I need a $1,000 check for these supplies out here." When that was taken care of, we sat down to look at the books. Horace came back in and I invited him to come and look too. Soon he was asking more questions than his wife. He had some very basic questions about Adam and Eve and sin that he felt were not being answered correctly at his church. I sat there and read him the whole chapter called, "The Price of Sin," from volume 1. He said, "I've never understood this before. This will really help me with my questions." They thought it would help them in teaching their teenage daughter as well.

He said he had a crew of men waiting for him about twenty miles away, but still he stayed, intrigued with *The Bible Story*. I pushed away thoughts of hurry. I thought, "This is more important than anything else he will do today." I showed him the *Bible Readings*, and he was even more pleased.

When they were considering the value of the books, I showed them my green sheet that shows how much people spend in bits and pieces for newspapers, pizza, sodas, etc. Horace leaned forward and said, "There's where I spend it—on sodas! I drink five or six of those a day. I never drink water, but I usually have a soda in my hand."

Bruce said, "That's interesting! You work to get water for people, but you don't drink it yourself!"

Horace replied, "That's right. I know I need to drink more water. I would feel better." Then he asked, "Would you mind if my wife made a copy of that sheet for me? I'd like to have that sheet to think about."

When I invited them to make a decision on the books, he talked with Molly for a moment, then said, "I think we should do it. Now if that's all you need me for, you can go ahead with the paperwork, and I'll go on to my men." I was glad the well driller had stayed and chosen to get the water of life.

Chapter 5

No One Ever Told Her Before

The lead card from Maria came with a white Post-it note written in broken English attached: *"Dear Sir: Please if you would contact me with a Spanish spoken person. I would like to obtain the children Bible in Spanish."* No street address was given, only a PO Box and a phone number.

I began calling the number in November in hopes that someone in the household would speak some English so I could make an appointment. It seemed fruitless. When her teenage daughter would answer the phone, Maria would be gone to work. When Maria or her husband answered, they couldn't understand English. Then the girl said they were going to Florida and wouldn't be back until early January. I stuffed the card into January in my appointment book and left it.

Around January 15 I tried again without success, but I couldn't get Maria off my mind. That Sabbath a retired couple in my church invited me to lunch. James was very interested in my canvassing work. He said if there was anything he could do to help me in my ministry to please let him know. The church I was attending was actually outside of my regular work territory, so I replied, "Just pray for me."

Suddenly it occurred to me what James could do. He is from Puerto Rico and his native tongue is Spanish. I said, "Oh, yes, I know what you can do. I have a card from a Spanish lady who wants *The Bible Story*. I need an interpreter."

James said, "Oh, I can help you. I was a Spanish translator in the United States Marine Corps."

By the next night, James had the appointment made for us to meet at 8:00 p.m. the following Thursday. I made sure I was sitting in my car near Maria's house on time that night. I watched for James to come as I waited and prayed.

At 7:50 a lady walked by with two bags of groceries. Our eyes met as she went by. She went to the house and went in. I wondered, "Is that Maria?"

At 7:58 a car pulled into the yard and parked. I wasn't sure if it was James, but at 8:01 I decided to find out. As I pulled into the driveway, I recognized his hat as he went up the steps. He turned and waved. I was amazed. We were on time and all there—three basic strangers with no direct communication since Sunday night!

They burst into a flood of joyful Spanish as we went in. She introduced us to her husband who was watching TV and then motioned us on into the next room. James and Maria kept on talking excitedly for the next several minutes. Then he turned to me and said, "We have established that what you say, I will repeat as if it is me talking to her, and what she says to me, I will repeat as if it is me talking to you. That will make it easier."

After a little exchange about family, work, and Maria's interest in the books, I pulled out my "World Falling Apart" notebook and began my presentation. Maria pulled her overstuffed chair closer and leaned forward. "*Si! Si!*" she said, nodding as I turned the pages and made my opening points.

When I handed her *The Bible Story*, volume 1, she smiled and said, "Yes, this is the book I look at when I'm at work in the clinic. It always draws me. Someone at work said, 'Why don't you send the card in so you can get these?' So, I did, and I have been waiting and thinking and thinking about these books. I am so glad you are here!"

She was leaning forward to catch everything we said. James was very good at interpreting, and he was right with me until I invited her to get her Bible to read about the animals going into Noah's ark in Genesis 7. Then they went into a three-to-five-minute session of Spanish that was a lot longer than the last sentence I'd said. I sat there holding in my laughter at my own helplessness. Finally, I said, "Remember, I can't understand anything you are saying."

James looked up and smiled, saying, "Oh, I was just explaining about the clean and unclean animals. "Oh, OK," I replied. Then we got back together on the presentation.

Maria loved the picture of Jesus and Nicodemus and the story of John 3:16. She loved the stories of Pentecost and of Paul and of Jesus coming again. She told me she looks at the *TV Guide* to find stories about Jesus, and they always make her cry. Her daughter says, "Why do you watch those if they make you cry?"

I showed her *The Desire of Ages* and said that if she is looking for a book about Jesus that will move her, this is such a book. I had James translate the paragraph, beginning, *"[Jesus] was treated as we deserve, that we might be treated as He deserves."*[1] Then they went into a session of extra Spanish words. Then I had him translate the paragraph about Jesus on the cross having pity for His tormentors.

Maria was moved. "I want this book!" she exclaimed.

When I presented the value, price, and procedures of how to obtain the books, Maria jumped up abruptly and left the room. We waited. In a moment she returned and put four twenty-dollar bills on the table for her down payment. She was ready to order!

When I finished writing her paperwork, James said, "Maria wants to tell you something: Thank you so much for coming and telling me all these stories. Thank you for taking the time. I wanted this for so long. You are the first person who has ever explained anything about the Bible to me!" That put tears into my eyes.

After signing her up for the *Discover Bible Guides* in Spanish and leaving a *Happiness Digest*, I asked James to pray. Maria instantly knelt, so we prayed, kneeling around her coffee table. When I reached out to shake hands and leave, this little woman threw her arms around me. She said I was helping her to be ready for heaven, and there we'll be able to talk!

> *Thank you so much for coming and telling me all these stories. Thank you for taking the time. I wanted this for so long. You are the first person who has ever explained anything about the Bible to me!*

---

1 Ellen G. White, *The Desire of Ages* (Mountain View, CA: Pacific Press, 1898), p. 25, emphasis mine.

Chapter 6

Seed Springing Up

"And he said, So is the kingdom of God, as if a man should cast seed into the ground; and should sleep, and rise night and day, and the seed should spring and grow up, he knoweth not how" (Mark 4:26-27).

I want to praise God for what He has done to fulfill this promise. When I met Maria and Juan in January, they knew so little English, and I knew so little Spanish, we had to have a translator for Maria to look at the books. Maria was very interested, but after a brief greeting, Juan went on with his TV program.

Maria placed her order for *The Bible Story* in Spanish and *The Desire of Ages*. Then the translator, James, talked further with her and offered her personal Bible studies in her home. She warmly agreed, and we went on our way. Later James told me that he and his wife had gone to visit these people, but I heard no more about it for nearly eight months. I prayed for Maria as I prayed for the rest of my growing flock as the months went by, and I thought of her whenever I passed through her town.

Near the end of August, I went on a trip to see my parents in Arkansas. When I returned, I found this message on my voicemail from James: "Maria and Juan are being baptized this Sabbath. Can you come?"

I was thrilled! While I was gone to Arkansas, telling colporteur stories at my parents' church, Maria and Juan were being baptized in Georgia. I called a friend about it, and she said, "Oh, yes, they were baptized, and sixty of their relatives and friends showed up. They've been coming to church for six to eight weeks now, and Maria just bubbles over with joy. When the minister gave the invitation at the end of the baptism, two more people came forward to ask for studies to be baptized. You must call Maria!"

So, I called her and her joy vibrated over the phone and broke the language barrier. She is so happy, rejoicing in Jesus! A week later I reached James. He told me, "Oh, yes, we studied with them, sometimes two or three hours at a time. They were so interested! They were just like sponges soaking up truth they had never heard before!"

Praise God for what He does while we sleep and rise and go on sowing the seed, sowing the seed, sowing the seed! And some of the seed comes springing up! His promise in Psalm 126:6 is that we shall doubtless come again with rejoicing, bringing our sheaves with us!

Chapter 7

All the Right Answers

The lead card from Dana came in flawless handwriting. Over several weeks we had already stopped by four times and not found her home. This time it was dark when we knocked. An attractive woman in a long-tailed T-shirt with long blonde hair opened the door. I said, "Hi! I'm Gladys Joy! And this is my husband, Larry. We got your little card about *The Bible Story*. Are you Dana?"

"Yes," she said. "This is a good time. I don't have to be anywhere else tonight. Please come in. Just give me a moment to make myself more presentable."

In a few minutes she was back, turning off the TV and settling her son Sam at the table in the next room with a bowl of cereal and milk. Then she sat down in the big recliner and said, "You don't mind if I keep this heating pad on my shoulder while we talk—I've pulled a muscle over the weekend."

As I shared why we do our work, Dana was in full agreement. She said, "Sam is only five, but he is different from my other children. He is very interested in books and loves to be read to. I don't want him to lose that. My other two are ages twelve and seventeen, and they don't want to sit down and read at all. They're into everything else."

Soon Sam came and curled up in Mommy's lap. When Larry spread out *The Bible Story* covers, Dana exclaimed, "Look, Sam! Look at all the pretty books! I didn't know there were so many of them!"

He looked, then turned over and went to sleep in her arms. Dana really liked what she saw. I shared about Paul and Silas singing in jail and read to her about the wound washer and how important it is to make things right when we've hurt someone.

I asked, "Do you like that?"

She said, "Oh, yes! Children can be so cruel. I talked to Sam just this morning on the way to school about always being careful not to hurt people by words we say."

I asked if she could see how these books would make a difference in her home.

She said, "Oh, yes! I wish I had done this for my older children when they were little; if I had, maybe they would be interested in the Bible now."

I had just closed *The Bible Story*, volume 10, and was reaching for the *Bible Readings* when Dana jumped and cried out, "Oh! A roach!" The two-inch-long bug was running full-speed toward my case. Larry quickly stomped on it. Dana shuddered and exclaimed, "I'm sorry. I don't do bugs well."

Larry said, "If you'll get me a tissue, I'll clean him up for you."

Dana carried her sleeping boy to his room, and Larry whispered, "Show her the *Bible Reference Library* for teenagers." I nodded.

She came back with a paper towel at arm's length in her fingertips, as if it already held the roach. She said, "I'll probably dream about roaches tonight." After that was done, she sat down again, now with both hands free to handle books and said, "OK, go ahead."

I asked, "Dana, do you like to read and study a lot yourself?"

> *She hugged The Desire of Ages and said, "I never knew about these before. These are wonderful!"*

She replied, "I don't read a lot. I'm not into novels, but I do like the Bible. It's kind of hard to understand, but I like this one I got at Walmart with comments by different people. I keep trying to read it through."

I said, "While we're here, let me just share the *Bible Reference Library* for teenagers and adults. It takes you all the way through the Bible again but on a deeper level."

Larry stretched out that spread, and Dana breathed, "Ohhhh!"

I told her that my dad had given me a set when I was fifteen, and I have read them over and over ever since. I showed her the *Bible Readings* and read several selections from *The Desire of Ages* and asked, "You can see how you would really use these if you had them, can't you?!"

She hugged *The Desire of Ages* and said, "I never knew about these before. These are wonderful! I'm glad my husband isn't here to stop me. He goes to church with us, but sometimes he doesn't understand how important these things are right now. He gets uptight about money, and when he gets uptight, it makes me get uptight. But we've always had a roof over our head and food in our mouth. God has never let us down. I really want this for Sam."

She seemed to be reasoning with herself. She added, "My middle child is my most expensive child. He's been in karate classes for four years. He just started on his black belt. There's a black belt with his name on it, and I'm on a contract paying sixty-five dollars a month till it's paid off. But he decided to drop out, and now he's into skating—speed skating with trips and tournaments. He has a big trip this weekend, and I'm still paying the sixty-five dollars a month for nothing. But this is different. Sam will use *The Bible Story*, and we'll go on using it. Sam will get his brother and sister to read to him when I can't. It will make a difference in my home."

I asked, "Dana, do you have a family Bible?"

She said, "No, but my grandmother used to have a big white one with all the pictures in it. I used to love to look at it." I showed her our *Family Bible* with its helpful features. She wanted one—white, of course, like Grandma's.

As I closed the paperwork, I asked if she had any more questions. "Just one," she replied. "When will my books get here?"

It seemed like an angel had stood by Dana's side with the list of all her objections and given her all the right answers!

Chapter 8

She Said, He Said, and God Did That!

Larry went to the front door with the lead card in his hand and met the lady of the house. She looked at it and said, "Oh, that's my husband. He's on the back porch. Just drive on around and you can see him back there."

So, he drove around and got out his case to go meet Lawrence. When Larry went up the steps and showed Lawrence the card, he said, "Oh, that's my wife. She sent that in. You can go in and show them to her."

Lawrence stepped in and called his wife to look. Then he went back out to visit with another friend on the porch while Larry showed her the *Bible Reference Library*. She liked the books, but when he explained price and asked her which way would work best for her to get them, she said, "Oh, I'll have to talk with my husband. I'm not working, and it'll be up to him."

Larry said, "Why don't you take some of the books out and show him and talk to him about it now." So, she did.

In a moment Lawrence came in with her. He asked, "So, how much are they?"

Larry explained the cost and payment options again.

He said, "Go ahead and get them. We'll do the monthly."

She said, "Well, I do get a disability check every month."

He said, "Don't worry about it. I'll find a way to pay for them."

Larry wrote the order, and came away, telling himself, "God did that! It wasn't me at all!"

Chapter 9

No Washing Machine!

Coming home after an apparently discouraging day, Larry found three phone messages on his machine. The first one gave a name and number and said, "I'm calling about the washing machine you advertised in the *Bargain Hunter*."

Larry mumbled, "I'm not selling a washing machine. There must have been a typo in the paper." The next message was similar, calling about the washing machine. He erased the messages and did not call them back.

The third message said, "This is Sheila. Please call me …."

So, Larry called.

When Sheila answered, she said, "Oh, yes, I was calling about the washing machine you have for sale."

Larry exclaimed, "But I don't have a washing machine for sale. That phone number must have been a typo in the *Bargain Hunter*!"

Sheila persisted, "So, do you have anything for sale?"

"As a matter of fact, I do," he replied. "I sell *The Bible Story*, those blue books you see in the doctors' offices."

Sheila said, "But all my children are grown."

Larry said, "Well, we have something really nice for adults called the *Bible Reference Library*. Would you like to look at those?"

She said she would, so they scheduled an appointment. The next day when Larry stopped by, he found that Sheila had a secondhand furniture store for the benefit of the poor. He showed her the books, and she ordered the *Bible Reference Library*.

Fast forward about nine years: We are having a moving sale and need to make space in the garage. A lady and her friend come to look at a table and some chairs. The lady is sitting in one of the chairs, deciding how much she's willing to pay. Larry walks in and sees her. He strides forward and exclaims, "Sheila!" and gives her a big hug. They talk like old friends. She tells him how she read her books and passed them on to her children.

They visit some more, and he sells her several more items, each with a little personal history, and we agree to deliver the furniture in a couple of hours. Sheila and her friend drive away with copies of *The Ministry of Healing*, *Happiness Digest*, and two copies of *The Ten Commandments Twice Removed*. When we pull into her driveway with the furniture later, she is sitting under a tree, reading the books. She tells us again how much she enjoys her books. We drive away, praising God again for Larry's *no washing machine*!

Chapter 10

Kelly—A Living Miracle

God has unique ways of getting me to show someone our books. For a week I had felt anxious about gathering all my tax forms, and I still needed one page. On my way to prayer meeting, I stopped at a house that advertised income tax services. A woman invited me in and asked what they could do for me. I told her I needed a Schedule C. She thumbed through a fat book of tax forms, found it, and said, "He can pull it off the Internet for you." She nodded toward a young man in a motor-propelled wheelchair. Other family members and friends were sitting around the room, visiting.

As Kelly wheeled over to his computer, his mom and I began to talk. She said her name is Marjorie. I asked if his condition is from a car accident.

"No," she replied, "Dirt bike and pickup truck."

As we stood by, watching the paper feed through the printer, she told me that when Kelly was twelve, he was in this accident. But that was not all: In a period of a few days, she had received several heavy blows in life.

First, her husband went into the hospital for some problems. About a week later he underwent surgery and some tests. A few days later Marjorie's daughter was in the hospital in another state giving birth to twins, and the family rejoiced over the announcement of the new boy and girl. At one o'clock the next morning they received a shocking call—the boy child had died.

About a week later Kelly was in the terrible, freak accident which rendered him a quadriplegic for life. In the middle of the intense struggle over Kelly's life and the long days of waiting in hospital corridors, Marjorie received the news of her husband's diagnosis. The doctor said Lou Gehrig's disease—four years to live.

Kelly looked up and asked in his whispery voice, "What kind of work do you do that you need a Schedule C?"

"Oh," I replied, "You know those blue Bible story books you see in the doctors' offices? My husband and I work for that company."

"Oh, yes," Kelly replied. "I like those books. I'd like to look at them sometime."

I said, "Let me go out and get a flyer from my truck for you. If you like, I'll come back tomorrow and show them to you." I brought him *The Bible Story* flyer, a *Bible Adventures Videos* flyer, and a *Happiness Digest*. We set up an appointment for noon on Thursday.

The printer went on to page 2, and Marjorie told me some more about her life. She said her husband lived for nine years after his diagnosis, being re-diagnosed with polymyositis, a form of muscular dystrophy. Just three years ago Marjorie had open heart surgery herself for a quadruple bypass. Yet here she is, caring for her handicapped son and trusting God to provide for them. She said, "I think God has just carried me most of the time through all this."

On Thursday Larry and I went back to show the books. Marjorie had more to tell me about Kelly and their experience. She said that the doctors gave her no hope for his life at the emergency room, but she told them, "As long as I have hope, you will put your hands on my child and work to save him!"

He came out of surgery fifteen hours later. The impact had battered him so much that every major organ was affected. One of his baby teeth had even been knocked down his windpipe and was embedded in one of his lungs. This mother held on in sheer courage, hope, and faith as her son lay in a coma from February until July. When others spoke doubt, she insisted, "God did not save my son's life on the operating table to let him die now. Even if he never wakes up, his life has been saved for a purpose!"

But Kelly did wake up that July, and his first words were, "Can I go to school tomorrow?"

That was nineteen years ago. Kelly did go back to school and went on to complete three degrees in college—his BA in General Business, and an AS in both Art and Science. Marjorie said with a smile that after the accident his mind wasn't quite as sharp. Before, he could read things once and have it memorized. Now he has to read things a second time and he's got it.

I showed them *The Bible Story* between pieces of their story. I was closing on *The Bible Story* with *Bible Readings* when Kelly whispered, "Do you have that book about Jesus? I saw it in the back of that book you left last night."

I pulled out the *Bible Reference Library* and read to him from *The Desire of Ages*. "Oh, I like that too," Kelly said. "I want to get that too." Again, I started to write the order, and again Kelly asked, "While you are here, could you just let me see the videos? I might like to get them later for my nieces and nephews."

I showed him the *Bible Adventure Video* set. His eyes shone as he placed his order for the twenty-two beautiful Bible volumes. "I will really enjoy these," he said. As we left, I praised God for sending me to that house for more than just a tax form. Their story had inspired me with hope and courage for my own life.

Chapter 11

From Disappointment to Divine Appointment

Here he was knocking on doors after dark in a rural community three days before Christmas. He had no orders yet and only twenty-five dollars in his bag for paperbacks. Larry really didn't feel like knocking on another door, but God helped him to go on. The first two houses were either not interested or not home, so he began riding through the neighborhood, looking for kids' stuff. He kept thinking of a house he'd seen earlier in the day with kids jumping on a trampoline. So, he went there and walked up with his survey clipboard.

A young woman named Linda invited him right in. Relatives were visiting. Linda had one of them get up and move so Larry could sit beside her on the couch and do his five questions. Then he asked Linda, "If you felt *The Bible Story* could help you in teaching your children and helping them make good decisions, would you like to look at our material?"

She gave a very positive "Yes!" and nearly followed him out to get his case. She said, "I just went to church last night for the first time in many years. I was thinking that I really need to be teaching my children these valuable lessons."

When Larry opened his case and started sharing the information, she kept telling things about her life that made him pull more books out of his case. Aunt Joan had plenty to say from her side of the room, and cousin Jessica had a few comments as well. One said, "The nice thing about the books is they're consistent. They'll always say the same thing!" They were having a fun time in a room full of talkers, but somehow the Lord brought them to the decision point on the books. By then Larry had showed Linda *The Bible Story, Bible Readings, Uncle Arthur's Bedtime Stories*, and *Train Up a Child*. She wanted it all. She said her little girl really likes to read.

He had just gone over the price with her when the phone rang. It was her husband calling. She started telling him who all was there. She turned to Larry and asked, "What was your name again?" Then she went on to her husband, "And Larry Bazemore is here with *The Bible Story*. I'm getting some books that will really help me in training the children."

Then she left the room to finish talking with her husband while the relatives went on visiting with Larry. When Linda came back, a momentary fear flashed through his mind that the order might be lost, but she was ready to sign the contract. She decided to put her deposit on a credit card, saying, "I'll just pay this off when the statement comes in."

It was one of those happy visits where Larry ministered to the people, and they ministered to him. Praise God that He can take our disrupted schedules and upset plans and hand us back a divine appointment!

> *Praise God that He can take our disrupted schedules and upset plans and hand us back a divine appointment!*

Chapter 12

Not a Cold Card

Not all of our old cards are cold cards. Some are still divine appointments! I met Marilyn in September, but she could not take the time to see me that day. She said her two grandchildren had just come in from school, and their mother had just walked off and left them and their father that very day. She was too upset about it to be able to look at the books. She asked me to hold onto her card for later, and that the best time and place to see her would be in the middle of the day at her workplace. She does bookkeeping at her husband's body shop in town.

Months passed, and we tried to contact Marilyn several times when we were in her area but could not connect. Then the last week of February, five months to the day from our first contact, we stopped at the body shop and she was just getting back from lunch.

She was glad to see me. She said she wondered if I had thought she was so rude in September that I might never come back. I told her I thought she was under a lot of stress, and I had kept her card, but we just hadn't connected again till now. "So, this is the day!" I assured her.

Her office was so tiny that Larry said he would go out and wait for me. Marilyn and I sat down, and she told me about her two grandchildren. The boy, age twelve, loves Jesus very much and is often reading his Bible, but he has cerebral palsy, and reading is hard for him. The girl, age ten, is a spelling whiz and has just won the school and district spelling bees. She is on her way to the state competition. "And she loves to read," Marilyn added. "They will both love these books."

She reached eagerly for each book as I made my presentation. At one point she stepped out into the shop for an interruption, but came back saying, "Oh, good, my husband is taking care of that man, so I won't have to stop while I'm getting my books."

She fingered the pages of the *Bible Readings* carefully, saying, "Oh, I didn't know about this book. This would even be good for a Sunday school class!" She was very pleased to order *The Bible Story* and *Bible Readings*.

As I did the paperwork, Marilyn said, "I didn't get the children anything for Valentine's Day. I was too tired that night, but they had enough candy and little junkie stuff for that anyway. But I told them I would find them something different this year—something really nice. This will be part of their Valentine's and last a lot longer."

When I asked if I could pray with her before I left, she said, "Oh, yes!" and reached out to take my hand. I prayed for God's blessing in her life and for strength and courage for the days ahead. As we opened our eyes, she began wiping tears away.

She said, "This morning I prayed, 'God, please send me someone to encourage me today,' and He sent you." It was a divine appointment not a cold card!

Chapter 13

I Was Expecting You!

At the end of a dirt road, I got out of our Blazer with an e-mail request for *The Bible Story* and *Bible Reference Library* in my hand. A big, shaggy black dog stretched and came down off the porch to meet me. A fluffy Pomeranian bounded out of the front door when Alexander, a retired gentleman, answered my knock. "Come on in," he said eagerly, "I was expecting you!"

Surprised and pleased, I stepped into the front room of the double-wide mobile home. He told me that the website indicated that someone would contact him in five or six weeks. I was amazed because I was on my way to another city, but I had felt it very urgent to stop in his town and locate a few leads on my way through.

Behind Alexander, I saw two elderly ladies in the kitchen, one on oxygen. He explained that they are his mother and sister. They went on to other activities as we spoke. Alexander said, "I want these for my grandson. I just want to know how much they are and how I can get them."

I explained that I carry some samples with me, and it only takes a few minutes to share those and answer his questions. "Just let me step out and get my case," I finished.

"Would you like some help?" he asked. "Can I carry anything for you?"

"Oh, thank you," I replied. "My husband and I usually work together and he carries it, but today he is working with our supervisor."

So, he carried in the case, and I spread out the covers for the two sets of books and began talking.

I learned that Alexander retired early on disability when he had two heart attacks ten years ago. He rejoiced as he recounted how God had provided over and over for him while he was obtaining his home even while he was getting onto disability pay. He showed me a photo of his two-year-old grandson, his pride and joy. He said, "I checked with his parents already to make sure there isn't a conflict with their beliefs, and I found out that these books are used by many denominations."

I smiled and asked, "What denomination is the Bible?"

He was very pleased as I showed *The Bible Story*, certain that it would really help his grandson to get to know God.

Then I shared the *Bible Reference Library*. When I read to him from *The Desire of Ages*, he said, "This will give me something to draw from when I make my articles for the newspaper. I try to put one in every week. This is really good!" When I invited him to order, he said, "You just got you a sale!" and went to get his checkbook.

I replied, "Praise the Lord! I'm glad you were home today and not gone to the doctor." He was also happy to sign up for the *Amazing Facts* Bible course before we prayed, and then he carried my case back out to the Blazer for me. I drove away joyful in the wonder of how God works, praying He would help me find others who are waiting and expecting me.

Chapter 14

He Shall Direct Thy Paths

I knew we would be working apart on Monday. Larry had his schedule and appointments worked out, but I was not sure where I should go. After he left, I studied the map and made my decisions. I thought I knew where I was going, but that hinged on getting a certain appointment. When I couldn't connect with that one on the phone, I prayed again about where to go.

We had the city of Baxley scheduled for Tuesday, but that plan had changed. But the Baxley area kept coming to my mind. I hesitated. Baxley is one of the points farthest from home. I was getting a late start. I was low on gasoline and low on money. But I could not think of any other town but Baxley. So, I prayed, "OK, Lord, I'll get gas and go to Baxley and trust You."

When I got there and located the first lead, it was way out in the country on a "pig path" in tall pines. No one was home there, and immigrants gathering pine straw on the property did not know when they would be back. I gave one of the men a copy of *El Centinela* (an outreach magazine) and went on. The rest of the afternoon I advertised, ran my other three leads, and knocked on some doors spontaneously. By 7:00 p.m. I had no orders and only twenty dollars for paperbacks. Then I remembered my first lead. I was glad I had found it in daylight because the mailbox had no number, and the driveway went at least a quarter mile through the woods.

Now Susan and Randy were home. They had arrived only twenty minutes before and were very interested in the books. Susan said, "They are for his children," and later she added, "We thought we should get these and be reading to them now while they are still young enough to listen because five years from now, forget it!" (The children are ages five, eight, and ten, and come to see Dad part-time.)

Randy is very loyal to his King James Version of the Bible, and Susan said they sometimes "got into it" in disagreement over that. But Randy said, "I love my Bible, but sometimes I don't understand all the words. If I get the *Bible Stories* and read them, I'll understand it better. My grandmother used to read these to me at the doctor's office, and I always wanted them."

"Yes," Susan added, "I always wanted some of these for my own."

She reached out to hold each book I took from my case. When I showed the *Bible Readings*, Randy reached for it too. "This will really help me," he said.

I asked if they both liked to read and study a lot. Susan said she does, so I invited them to look at our Bible stories for adults—the *Bible Reference Library*—and they were really excited over these too. When I explained cost and paperwork, they were thrilled at how economically our books are priced.

Randy said, "When I saw those adult Bible stories, I knew I wanted them, too, but I didn't know if I could do it all right now. We can handle this!"

Susan wrote out the deposit check and said, "We've been eliminating debt, and we're nearly all caught up now, so we didn't do anything for each other this year for Christmas." Then they looked at each other and said, "Merry Christmas!"

Before I prayed with them at the end, I told them it was not a coincidence that I was in their home, but that I felt God had led me to Baxley for them that day. I told them how I had prayed many times for guidance and that He had kept me delayed until they got home.

"Yes," they said. "We know He did because when we came home, we were locked out of our house, and we had to go get our extra key from our neighbor down the road. Besides, we are not going to be here tomorrow."

I left them with joy in my heart that God had directed my paths—even down a "pig path."

Chapter 15

Golf Carts or Heat Waves

The e-mail request from George led us to a nice country home. A child's swing set and gym were in the backyard, and three small yapping dogs poured out of the empty garage to meet us. Larry said, "I don't think anybody is home, and these little ankle-biters are the ones that will get you!"

"Right," I replied, "and there's a big, black one back in the corner."

Larry adjusted his gaze from the bright sunshine to the shadows of the garage where an extra-large Rottweiler stood, barking at us. "Let's come back this evening," he concluded.

We went on and found Hannah, a simple country woman in a humble, single-wide trailer. She was on disability and couldn't order today, so I offered her our little books and a children's magabook. She asked, "Could I get this whole mess for twenty-five dollars?" She was very excited. She exclaimed, "I can't believe you are standing here! I've tried to get some of these books for years!"

Later that afternoon we met Dee, an enthusiastic woman who also wanted *The Bible Story* for her nine grandchildren. The gnats were getting bad outside, so when she invited us in, Larry replied, "Thank you! I'm sure there are fewer gnats in there!"

We sat in her crowded sitting room to show her the books. I could feel the sweat streaming down inside my clothes as her fan circulated the hot, humid air. Dee told us how she had decided to put her whole trust in God. She said, "I have no kidney. I go to dialysis three times a week."

Her kidney transplant didn't take. She is diabetic and on insulin. She had been through three different kinds of depression medication and suffered many bad side effects. She said, "One day I was tired of it. I took all the medication and flushed it down the commode. I said, 'God, either

You are God, or You are not. Either You can keep me alive or You can't. I'm just going to trust You and praise You."

So, she did. She still goes to dialysis regularly, but she has energy and cooks and takes care of her family. She said, "God still has me here for some reason. She took our little set and three magabooks. Glowing with confidence, she said, "When the praises go up, the blessings come down!"

Back outside, the heat was still in the upper 90s. I threw my shoulder bag in the back of our vehicle so I could get to the air conditioning as soon as possible. I felt like I was melting! We drove back to George's house. This time we found two vehicles in the garage, but all was quiet—even the dogs were missing! Larry said, "Maybe they're out walking. It's cooling off a little."

As we turned away to go, I said, "Could you wait a moment? I didn't reload my bag at the last place. Could you fill it up for me?"

Suddenly I was aware of someone behind me. I turned to see a golf cart with a six-year-old at the wheel and his mother beside him. They had puzzled looks on their faces.

I walked over and asked, "Is George home tonight?"

She said, "Yes. He's out back hitting golf balls. We'll go get him."

She took the e-mail request, and they drove away as quietly as they had come. In a few minutes they were back with all the dogs tagging along.

George said he had sent the e-mail about *The Bible Story* because his mother had them when he was little, and he wanted them for his son. "Come on in where it's cool," he added.

At their dining room table with *The Bible Story*, George said, "We're looking for something for devotional material on a child's level. We've tried reading right out of the Bible, but that's not working for us."

Todd climbed into Lou's lap and asked, "Mom, do we get to keep those today?"

She said, "No, we're going to get you your own set." Then I shared the *Bible Reference Library*, and Lou said, "Those are really nice. We should get them too."

When they were ready to order, George asked Lou, "How do you want to do it?"

She asked, "How much do you have? I think we should just pay cash for it."

When I handed George the paperwork and thanked him for his order, he said, "I had my mind pretty well made up before you came."

We told them we were so glad we found them home that day. I said, "We just paused to refill my bag or we would have missed you!"

Lou replied, "And Todd kept on wanting to drive the golf cart back up to the house or we would have missed you!" God really has amazing timing tools—even heat waves and golf carts!

Chapter 16

From Office to Parking Lot

The lady's purse was on top of *The Bible Story* book in the doctor's office. "Pardon me," I said. "Could I get that blue book and check it?"

She lifted her purse and I took the damaged book. I put a new book on the table and her husband promptly picked it up, saying, "I always wondered how to get these books. I've seen them around since my children were small, and now I've got great-grandchildren." We talked for a few minutes and he filled out a lead card.

I saw from the card that they were from another town, so I asked, "Will you be waiting here long? Would you like for my husband to show you the books now? He's sitting out there in the lobby."

Irene said to Clarence, "You go look at the books. I'll wait here for the children." Clarence got right up and went out with me.

I said, "Larry, this is Clarence. He would like you to show him the books while I finish this building." They shook hands and went out together to get our case.

Thirty minutes later when I came off the elevator, I found them all in the entryway. Larry was on his knees showing the books. Clarence and Irene were sitting on a little bench, and the two wiggly little girls were walking back and forth, activating the automatic doors. Besides the children, office workers were going in and out during their lunch break, so the big sliding doors were heaving open and shut the whole time Larry was talking. With all that action going on,

> *This divine adventure ended in the bank's parking lot a few miles away with prayer and a Bible course enrollment. We parted with all of us rejoicing in the Lord!*

Clarence and Irene stayed focused on the books. I'm sure the angels were helping them.

Larry had just finished showing them *The Bible Story* and was spreading out the *Bible Reference Library* when I arrived. Larry asked if Clarence taught a Sunday school class. He said, "No, but they would like me to."

From childhood Clarence was taught the value of following the Lord and had tried to pass these values on to his children. When Larry gave the invitation, he was ready to order the full 22-volume set. There was just one problem—they didn't have their checkbook with them. After a short discussion, they said, "Just follow us to the bank so we can get our deposit."

This divine adventure ended in the bank's parking lot a few miles away with prayer and a Bible course enrollment. We parted with all of us rejoicing in the Lord!

Chapter 17

Today I Was Praying and You Came!

It was dark and cold as I left Larry at his appointment and got back into the car, fumbling for the ignition. I prayed, "Father, please help me. I don't know this town very well, but it is only ten minutes to 8:00, and we really haven't seen many people or written any orders yet today. Please make me effective in this last hour. Give me somebody who is looking to heaven for light."

I drove down the street and pulled in at the first house. The lady there was cordial but not interested. At the next corner I paused. Where to go, Lord? Which house? A vehicle was coming, so I pulled ahead to a house with lights on and pulled into the narrow driveway. To my dismay the other vehicle paused with its blinker on for that driveway. I decided to back out and get out of the way. When I did, the young woman pulled partway in, opened her window, and spoke. I struggled to open the correct window on our car, pushing all the other buttons first before my window opened. She asked, "Do you need directions? Are you from around here?"

I answered, "No, I am working with *The Bible Story* library. I just have a hard time with my husband's car because I'm used to driving my Blazer. I'm visiting some parents in the area with a little survey on family values." Our two vehicles were completely blocking the narrow street. The thought flashed in my head, "Let go of your embarrassment. Invite her to look at the books."

I said, "Would you like to pull ahead, and I'll pull in after you, so you can do the survey?"

"OK," she replied.

As she walked back up the drive, she said, "Come on in, and I'll go see if my husband is OK with this. He's in the back room with our son."

We walked into a big empty front room with a few boxes along the walls. She explained, "We just moved in a couple of months ago, so there's no furniture out here yet."

In a moment they were both inviting me back to the cozy kitchen and dining room. I could see their curiosity change to spiritual interest as I did the survey and pulled out *The Bible Story* flyer. Terry handed Eileen the baby and took the flyer, browsing through it thoughtfully. I invited them to take a few minutes and look at our materials. They decided to look, and as I got my case I prayed, "Lord, they need a miracle, and I need a miracle."

We sat down at the kitchen table and got acquainted. Baby Frank was six months old, and his Daddy, Terry, works at the family business which is one of the major industries in the area. I asked Eileen if she worked out of the home or if she gets to be with her baby. She hugged the baby and said, "No, we are really blessed. I get to be home with him, and he is such a good baby. He's never sick and we have such a good time." They had the baby on a schedule, and we paused in our discussion so she could feed him and put him to bed on schedule.

Both Terry and Eileen were intrigued as I showed them the stories of Adam and Eve, and Noah, and shared the plan of redemption. She said they would learn a lot from these themselves. Terry was especially interested because he does not have as much free time to attend Bible study classes as Eileen.

When I asked for the order, Eileen hesitated and brought up the expenses of just getting their house. I saw a look of conviction cross Terry's face and he said, "Could we just go and talk this over for a minute?"

When they came back, Terry said they would like to do just *The Bible Story* and *Bible Readings* for now, and then call me for the rest of the books after they were more settled in their home.

Terry paused then said, "I am really amazed that you came to our house. Today I was praying that God would give me some structured way to learn the Bible. Church and preaching are OK, but I really want to know these stories and be able to share them with my son. So, I was praying, and then you came."

Then Eileen asked, "Aren't you going to tell her what you told me?"

Terry paused then said, "I am really amazed that you came to our house. Today I was praying that God would give me some structured way to learn the Bible. Church and preaching are OK, but I really want to know these stories and be able to share them with my son. So, I was praying, and then you came."

I said, "We stopped by the road and prayed today more than once for God to lead, and you know how Satan tries to keep things from happening. He tried to make me feel embarrassed when I pulled into your driveway."

Eileen said, "I don't usually pull right up behind people, but someone broke into my vehicle right in the driveway not long ago, so I was checking you out when you pulled in." She felt very apologetic. "We are so glad you came. God sent you."

I prayed for them before I left, and Terry carried my case out to the car, praising God again for what He had done.

If you question your work for God when you are struggling to pay your own bills or trying to deal with your own troubles, remember this: There are still people out there, looking to heaven for light, praying for answers, waiting for someone to knock on their door.

Chapter 18

What Took You So Long?

We knocked on Sherry's door in Valdosta. When she saw the blue card for *The Bible Story*, she said sharply, "What took you so long? I sent that card in months ago! Why didn't you come before?"

We explained apologetically that we have no regular representative in her area, and we were just filling in for a few days. Her husband Peter came in to look at the books with her. Their two-year-old daughter "bounced off the walls" while Larry showed the books, but nothing could break their interest. After placing their order, they slipped to their knees when Larry offered to pray with them. They were so glad we had come.

For four days we worked the Valdosta area from lead cards that were two to six months cold. Every day there were special people looking for hope—some in beautiful homes, some in squalor and filth—all with spiritual needs. Then we drove the 150 miles back home to work our regular area.

A month passed, and the waiting lead cards from deep South Georgia were on our hearts again. We called the Waycross pastor and arranged a place to stay. We left our regular twenty or so counties and went. This trip was different. Leads were farther apart. We drove miles and miles to find them. Some could only buy paperbacks; some could do less. But some could order.

On our last demo Lena invited us into her new double-wide home—so new it had been delivered just two days before, and they were moving in. Lena had *The Bible Story* as a child. She had read them through. She wanted them for her baby girl. She could hardly let me say any of my presentation. She wanted to know how much and how to get them right now!

When I put the *Bible Readings* into her hands and just turned a couple of pages, she excused herself for a moment. When she returned, tears were pouring down her face. She did not say why. She got her business checkbook and wrote the deposit. She did not want audible prayer but asked us to pray for her later on our own. Her lead card was four months old. People are still waiting. Who will go?

Chapter 19

To Find Titus

It was a very small town, and we had six leads that were all post office box addresses. We prayed God would give us the right people to help us with directions. At city hall a clerk and the mayor herself looked through the cards and identified two or three and gave us directions. They weren't sure about Franklin or Titus, but they said, "If you go to the church by the highway on the east end of town, the people living in trailers across the street there might know them."

We worked on in the rain, following the sketchy directions, leaving a *Happiness Digest* here and there and a few Bible course cards. Finally, we headed for the church on the end of town, wondering who would help us to find Franklin or Titus. A young man came down the sidewalk from the trailers. Larry pulled over, and I asked through my open window, "Do you know Franklin or Titus?"

He replied, "I'm Franklin, and Titus is my first cousin." I held out *The Bible Story* lead card, and he said, "I sent that in. I like reading them." But he was not employed now, so he took a *Happiness Digest* and a Bible course card.

Directing us to Titus, he pointed across the main highway and explained, "Take that street straight behind you and go till you can't go any more. Turn left. You'll see some blue and white apartments. Go past them. There are some brown apartments behind them. Write this down, 2E. He is in the brown apartments at 2E."

We thanked him and headed for 2E. There we found Titus, a young man sharing the apartment with his mother and his teenage daughter. He wanted *The Bible Story* for his seven-year-old son. His mother Lois had a Bible in her hand as she invited us in. Titus said he had to leave in fifteen minutes for school. He is working on his GED after fourteen years out of school. For a moment it seemed that time pressure would cheat them out of the opportunity to consider eternal things. But Titus asked us to sit down and show him the books.

Lois held her open Bible in her lap. As Larry shared about Noah and the animals going into the ark, they were both amazed to learn about the sevens and the twos. Larry pointed out how Noah showed his faith in Jesus, the Lamb of God that takes away the sin of the world, when he sacrificed one each of the clean animals. Then he turned back to the story of Genesis 3:15 about the Seed of the woman who would crush the serpent's head. When Larry mentioned going through the set in a year by reading a story a night and two on Sundays, Lois said, "But we only have him on weekends!"

"Then you'll have to read more stories!" Larry responded with a smile.

Looking at the picture of Jesus coming again, both Titus and Lois said they think it will be soon. Titus' teenage daughter walked through the room, and he told her, "These will be for all of us. You'll get to read these too!" Lois asked Titus about school today, and he said, "I'll just do an hour tonight. It's just math today anyway."

As Titus placed his order for the *Bible Readings* and New Testament portion of *The Bible Story*, he said, "I was on break at the hospital and something impressed me to pick that book up and read it instead of the magazines there. That's when I found the card." He said when he saw us coming up the walk he had said, "Here come some of God's people. Somehow I always recognize my real brothers and sisters."

He hugged Larry and gave me a warm handshake after our prayer together. We left with a renewed sense of awe for the God we serve, who knows where all His children are all the time, who delayed us and directed us all day long to find Titus at 2E.

CHAPTER 20

Recycling God's Precious Treasures

The letter from our old friend said, "I found a set of *The Bible Story* at Goodwill ... I've got them for you for the poor. Come by and pick them up ...."

We stopped at Bernice's house the next day and had a nice visit. Only volume 6 was missing. She said, "I wondered if I should get them or leave them there for someone who really needs them."

I thanked her for getting them and said, "Sometimes it takes a colporteur to get people to recognize how valuable the books are and to help them see their spiritual need. We do meet people who are in very extenuating circumstances who would love to get their hands on an old set of these books." Before we left, we prayed together that God would help us place these old treasures in the right home. Then we went on working.

At our last visit that evening we met Mila, a single mom with three very nice children, who lives in a government housing project. She drives a van for a medical transport organization. While waiting for a patient at a renal dialysis center, she had read through a sample of *The Bible Story* book. She thought the books would really help explain the Bible to her children, so she e-mailed in her request for information. She said, "I wasn't raised in a church, so I didn't learn these stories. When I was older my mom joined the Jehovah's Witnesses church, so that's my background." She really liked what I showed her, and her eight-year-old boy sat right beside her and listened the whole time. He really wanted those books.

I was sure that Mila would not have the resources to purchase the set or commit to a monthly payment, but I went through the process of inviting her to order and probing for her objections so I could find out how much she wanted the books. I could see the disappointment mounting on her face. When we determined that she could not even handle a half set, I asked Larry if he had anything to say. He had been waiting for my question with a twinkle in his eye. He turned to Mila and inquired, "If you could get most of these books tonight for your children for just twenty-five dollars, would you do it?"

"Just twenty-five dollars?!" Mila exclaimed, her face lighting up. "Oh, yes! I could do that!" Then we told her we had obtained a used set in beautiful condition with only one volume missing, and we'd be glad to leave it with her for twenty-five dollars. She turned to her teenager and said, "Go get me my purse!"

When Larry carried in the books, the family gathered around and the eight-year-old reached for his favorite—volume 4, David and Goliath. Larry said, "You've got a real treasure here!"

After we prayed together, Mila said, "You have just made my day! Last night the mother of one of my friends died, and today has been really hard. Thank you so much!"

When we reached out to shake hands, she stepped forward and gave us each a hug. Later that night I called Bernice to tell her what happened to those books. She was thrilled that God had used her to recycle some of His precious treasures.

Chapter 21

A Real Investment

We were running some old leads in a military town beyond our regular territory. Kay's card showed that she lived on the base, but the street was not showing on our map or on the GPS. So, I called her. I felt embarrassed to have to explain that we have no regular representative in her area, and that is why no one had responded to her card for two or three years. When Kay realized I was calling about *The Bible Story* lead card, she began to laugh. It had been so long since she sent the card; she had given up hope of a response. But she was still interested and told us to come. She said, "I'm not doing anything today but laundry, so I'll be here."

When we arrived, we found Grandma, Kay, and one of her two girls at home. As Larry opened his case, Kay said, "We're Adventists. We used to live in North Carolina, and the church there gave me a really old set of *The Bible Story*, but a lot of the pages are missing, so we're missing those stories."

She shared some of their experiences with the church, and Grandma had a running commentary. Grandma was sad and somewhat bitter over the loss of four of her five children to illnesses and accidents. She said she had buried them all but Kay and paid all those expenses. She seemed quite disappointed in life itself.

Kay asked if we had any videos or DVDs. Larry pulled out *My Bible Friends* and *Quigley Village*. Kay said her husband George would be home soon. He is a medic and was heading for Iraq in two weeks. I could see that Grandma was running interference with everything Larry presented to Kay. Kay had seated herself on the rug and turned to me several times to apologize for Grandma's negative onslaught. By this time there were *My Bible Friends*, *Bedtime Story* books, and *The Bible Story* in Kay's hands and across the floor, and a *Quigley Village* running on the TV for the four-year-old. But Grandma and Kay were engaging Larry in too much conversation about church and family to really focus on the books.

I reached out to Kay and said, "Let me show you what you have in that *Bedtime Story* book." She handed it over, and I methodically walked her through the features—lesson index, story themes, illustrations, and activity pages.

With each feature, Kay gave an indication of delight. She asked, "Are there this many stories in every book?"

"Oh, yes!" I assured her. I reached for *The Bible Story* next. She was very pleased with the Bible references at the beginning of the stories.

As I showed her the lesson on obedience in the Adam and Eve story, she said, "This is nice. These pages are missing in my old set."

At the page in the "World Falling Apart" notebook which shows the boy with the gun, I asked, "You want to protect your kids from ever being in this picture, don't you?!"

Kay replied, "Oh, yes! That's all around us here. There are gangs here on the base, and kids are shooting in the streets."

George came in as I was finishing with volume 10. He stood there in his army fatigues, watching for a moment before changing clothes. He came back as we were going over the *Bible Reference Library*. By now both little girls had joined us and were trotting in and out of the room, nibbling on apples.

Kay was very interested as we looked at the *Triumph of God's Love*. Grandma had said they already had a big *Bible Readings*, and Kay had showed me the very small copy of *Patriarchs and Prophets* they were reading. When I asked if they had any questions, they said, "How much for everything?"

They were pleased when I showed them the numbers and said it would work for them. George said, "It's an investment in my kids!"

Grandma asked what the balance and the monthly would be, and then added her blessing, saying, "It's a real investment!"

When we stood for prayer, Kay asked to be remembered as she was facing serious surgery in a few weeks. I praise God for these parents. They could have said, "We're facing surgery. We're facing deployment. It's not a good time." But they looked at their children's future instead and said, "It's a real investment!"

Chapter 22

The Trapper

Every time we pass Merlin's place, I think of the visit we made there on Christmas Eve several years ago. His house is tucked away on a dead-end street below the bank of a four-lane highway. We found him in the backyard at a worktable, scraping the inside of an animal hide. We asked if he had time to look at *The Bible Story*, and he said, "Oh, yes! Just let me wash my hands first!" He pulled the hide off the board and flipped it right side out, and there was a perfect coonskin.

As he led us into his house, he explained that he hunts and traps in partnership with Wildlife Management for the area and supplies skins to the Indian trading post people for making their crafts. Finished animal skins of fox, beaver, and coons hung near the door, and the living room was decorated with Indian art. A mounted bobcat had its shelf above the fireplace.

Merlin told us that his wife had an Indian heritage, but she had been killed in a tragic auto accident not long before as she pulled onto the four-lane highway. He was left alone, raising their three children. He said he takes his oldest with him on his hunting excursions to keep him away from wrong associations. Merlin wanted *The Bible Story* for his children for Christmas and also as a resource for his involvement at his church. He asked if there was any way that he could get a set in time for Christmas. He was ready to pay cash. We had a set at home, so we were able to deliver the books that night. After that we always thought of him as we passed by.

This week we were down the street from Merlin's, and Larry said, "Maybe we ought to stop by and see how he's doing."

"Let's do," I replied.

Merlin met us at the door. Larry asked, "Do you remember us?"

"Yes," he smiled, "you sold me some books years ago."

"We think about you whenever we drive by on the highway," Larry said. "How are you doing?"

Merlin was glad to come out on the porch and visit. He told us he had chosen not to remarry but to give himself more fully to the Lord and involvement in service to Him. He was out of regular work but had odd jobs going in the community that generate income. "The Lord always comes through," he said. "I have my last child attending Georgia Military College now."

Merlin is still teaching Sunday school at his church and doing things to involve others in outreach. He said that when his children were still at home, he would gather them around in the evenings and read *The Bible Story* to them. It seemed to pull the family together. Now he uses the books as resource study material for his teaching. As the men talked in the deepening twilight, I looked around at the tools and equipment on the porch. A basket under the window held a cat with her tiny kittens.

Larry showed him our little books and told him they are from our adult set of *The Bible Story*. Merlin was glad to get them. He pulled out a twenty-dollar bill, saying, "I can afford these. They will help me in my studies." We had a prayer together and shook hands as the stars were coming out. "I'm glad you came by right now," he said, "I was just about to go somewhere when you drove up." We were glad too—glad to know what God is doing through His books and through the trapper.

Chapter 23

Spontaneous Joy!

God wants to do more for us than we ever imagined, and some days He takes me by surprise! On Tuesday, February 24, 2004, I was working alone while Larry worked with our district leader, Bruce. I could not get an early start because of my list of morning commitments: buying and mailing out a little Baptist hymnal to one of my eighty-year-old customers (That's another story!), picking up my new glasses and having them fitted, and having an overdue oil change done on my Blazer. By 12:30 I was free to start advertising, and by 1:00 p.m. I was finally on the road to Rochelle to canvass and to keep my 6:00 p.m. appointment with Bill and Angie, whom I was teaching to read.

I looked at my gas gauge—not really low, but less than half a tank. I had no cash and less than two dollars left of visible money in the checking account. I was sure God would give me cash for paperbacks as I knocked on doors in Rochelle, but for some reason, I felt overly nervous about going that far with no cash and not enough gas for the round trip. I was determined not to put gas on our bulging credit card. So, I pulled into a neighborhood and started knocking. The first house did the survey and took one free tract. Then I saw two ladies and a toddler walking up to the next house. I pulled in so I could talk to them before they went inside. They were a mom and grandmother with the fifteen-month-old toddler.

Nita was instantly interested in the survey, and when I offered to show her *The Bible Story* books, she said, "I always wanted some of these. Come in."

She told me that she is a manager at a McDonald's in another town. This was not her house but her aunt's; she lived down the street. I think they came by to check on her uncle who sat there in a wheelchair. As I showed the books, Nita, her mom, and her uncle were all interested. The baby kept coming to me for her share of attention, holding up her little hands.

When I showed Nita the *Train Up a Child* book, she looked through it very carefully. She said, "This will help me so much!"

She and her mom agreed to "go halves" on *The Bible Story, Bible Readings,* and *Train Up a Child*. Her mom went down the street to get the main part of the deposit while the uncle went to his room to get the rest. Nita told them, "I'll pay you back when I get paid this afternoon." I looked up from the paperwork to see tears running down Nita's face. She said, "I know God knows where I am."

She was so glad I came. I believe I was sent. When I left, I wrote a check exchange to put with her order and dropped her deposit in the bank. Then I started out for Rochelle. I felt better!

It was about 2:00 p.m., and I had about seventy-five miles to go. About fifty miles later I came to the last major highway junction before Rochelle. It's really just a wide spot in the road with a C-store on one side and an old house on the other. I saw a car at the house and decided to stop since I'd never stopped there before. A woman was on the porch. She was glad to do the survey and invited me in. Her children were grown, but she wanted to understand the Bible better for herself. She decided to start with just *Bible Readings* and the Old Testament part of *The Bible Story* since she's only working part-time right now. Again, God surprised me with an order but no small, cash books.

I drove the remaining twenty some miles to Rochelle and located the street where I had left off last time. When I went up and knocked on the house, a woman got out of a white truck that was parked out front. She called, "She's not home yet, but she'll be here in a few minutes."

I walked out to her and started to talk. She said, "My fan belt tore up. My friend lives here. She doesn't know it yet, but she is giving me a ride home. I don't trust this vehicle to get me there." She lifted the hood and showed me the disintegrating belt. "I just had this put on last night," she added.

I invited her to do the survey and she said, "But I don't have any kids." I replied, "But you have opinions, and that's all it's about." So, she agreed, and we started in.

I had just handed Ruth *The Bible Story* flyer when her friend, Joanne, drove up. Joanne was very interested, and they had both read the books in doctors' offices. Joanne said she had been working on Ruth for ten years to go to church with her, and Ruth had just started going. They were really good friends.

Joanne apologized that she couldn't invite me in because she had just torn the house up with remodeling. I told them that was OK; the hood of the truck would be a good table. So, we stood there at the truck with books and papers spread out all over. They loved the books.

Joanne said her small son had gone through intense separation anxiety when she put him in day care and went to work. She said, "It's better now, but we still have a behavior problem." I made sure to include the *Train Up a Child* book.

As they decided what to do, Ruth asked if she could start with part of the books, and Joanne asked what her payments would be if she put $250 down. I wrote Joanne's order first: *The Bible Story, Bible Readings*, and *Train Up a Child*. Then I did the one for Ruth: The *Bible Readings* with the Old Testament part of *The Bible Story*.

Ruth said, "I don't know why my truck tore up again today."

I told her, "Why, it was so you could get these books!"

She and Joanne laughed in agreement. They were full of plans for using the books. I was full of joy as I drove away to my 6:00 p.m. appointment with still no cash for small books but perfect assurance that God wanted me to have spontaneous joy instead of cash!

When Larry and I talked at the end of the day, I learned that God had given him spontaneous joy with cash! He and Bruce had written two spontaneous orders for *The Bible Story* and *Bible Readings* plus knocking on doors until they received over $100 in small donations for our little books. Praise God for His spontaneous joy!

Chapter 24

Three Divine Appointments

As we headed for Homerville, I said, "Oh, Larry, there's a lead somewhere along this highway. Want to watch for the number?" Soon we found the house, and there we found Beverly. She had e-mailed a request about the *Bible Reference Library*. Beverly was dealing with grandchildren, so she turned us over to her husband Ben. She said, "You look at these, honey. I've got to take care of the girls. They were having a "girls' weekend" for their five granddaughters. Next time it would be a "boys' weekend" for their four grandsons. In a few minutes they were leaving to take all the girls back to their parents.

Ben invited us to sit down with him at the kitchen table. He said he always loved reading *The Bible Story* in the doctor's office. Now he wanted them for his grandchildren. Larry shared *The Bible Story/Bible Reference Library*. Ben was retired from the railroad after thirty-nine years and change. Beverly had retired after many years at a container manufacturer. Now they each have a part-time job and a lot more time to do what they want.

When Larry asked for the order, Ben hesitated and deferred to his wife. "She's the bookkeeper," he said. Beverly studied the sales sheet that showed the savings when getting the two sets together. Then she said, "You've always wanted these. You always look at them at the doctor's office and say you wish you could get them. Let's go ahead and do it now. How much is that deposit?" She got out her checkbook and reached for the paperwork. It was a divine appointment on a Sunday afternoon.

We puzzled over an address; then we found it was an attorney's office. A car was there, and the lawyer himself opened the door when we rang the bell. Tim explained, "I'm just getting a head start on tomorrow." But he had time to look at *The Bible Story* for his granddaughter.

As Larry showed Tim the books, I sat across the room on a leather chair and looked at our surroundings. The big desk was stacked high with file folders and papers. On the walls I counted over thirty impressive certificates, and through an open door many fat law books lined the shelves. Tim talked about some of his own evangelistic speaking and said he had worked on law cases of people who had died and revived on the operating table who told him they had gone through the tunnel, but Jesus had sent them back, saying it wasn't their time yet.

Tim said he would have to discuss the purchase of the big set with his wife, but when Larry offered him our pocket edition set, he gave an eager, "Yes!" and reached for his wallet. We were glad because he really needed those books! It was another divine appointment.

Then there was Nancy on Thursday. As I refilled the flyers and checked the books at one waiting room, a woman spoke to me. "I've been wondering how I could get one of those Heritage Bibles. I took a flyer home once, but I lost it. Do you know how to get one?"

"Yes," I replied. "I sell those. I have one out in the car. Are you waiting for someone? Would you like to look at it?"

"My mother is in with the doctor," Nancy said. "Yes, I would like to see it."

I went to the car and brought back the Heritage Bible, *Bible Readings*, and a contract pad. No other patients came in as I showed her the books. Our only interruptions came from Nancy's one-year-old baby girl as she played around the room. When I invited Nancy to order, she went out to her car to get her debit card. I asked her if she believed in divine appointments. She replied, "Yes."

I said, "We just had one!"

Chapter 25

The Sheep in the Bank

We were praying for God to help us find His sheep as we ran leads in open territory. We arrived in another little town just before noon and went to the chamber of commerce to get a map. A note on the door said, "Gone to lunch. Back at 2:00." Spotting a bank up the street, we pulled in there. As we walked in, we saw two *The Bible Story* books on a small table. Larry said, "See if they have cards in them."

I stopped to check. Both books had cards, so I took one of the books with me to Vanessa's desk where Larry was waiting for a map. Seeing the blue book, she asked, "How do you get those? I had my baby recently, and I sent a card in six weeks ago, but I haven't heard anything back. Do they send something in the mail?"

Larry replied, "We provide a personalized service. We don't have a regular representative in this area right now, so we are filling in. Could we come by and visit with you after work?"

She had an appointment after work, so I asked, "Do you have a lunch break?"

Two hours later we sat in Vanessa's office, and I prayed for no interruptions as Larry showed her the books. She had spent ten years in the Navy in communications on ship and now enjoyed her work as a bank officer back in her hometown. She said she is already reading to Tanya because she thinks it is important—even though Tanya would rather grab the book and bite it right now since she is teething.

> *When we offered to pray with her, she held out her hands. We were so glad God knew His "sheep" was in this bank and would respond when we gave the invitation.*

Larry asked, "If you felt you could help Tanya make good decisions, to be obedient and respectful, to protect her from drugs and crime, and most of all to give her heart to Jesus, by providing *The Bible Story* for her, would you do that?"

Vanessa threw her hands open and exclaimed, "Yes! That's why I sent the card in!" *(We love it when people answer that emphatically!)*

Larry quickly showed her the features of the books, ending with the painting of Jesus coming again in the *Bible Readings*. He asked, "How do you like what I've shown you? Would you use these if you had them?"

She said, "I don't know why anybody wouldn't want them!"

Vanessa dug in her purse for her checkbook. She laughed as she said, "I used the last check in both of my accounts when I paid my bills yesterday. I'll just have to walk out there and get a counter check." In a minute she was back with cash for the deposit. When we offered to pray with her, she held out her hands. We were so glad God knew His "sheep" was in this bank and would respond when we gave the invitation.

Chapter 26

Thank You for All the Prayers

In John and Tammy's home we found two professional career parents: one, a teacher of agriculture, the other, a registered physical therapist. The house oozed "Success!" Their twenty-month-old toddler, Gabe, was wrapped in bandages from a severe burn. As the parents hesitated to order *The Bible Story* books, we learned that Gabe faced major corrective heart surgery in the near future and that student loans made a big shadow of debt over this mother's desire to be home with her child.

She objected over money to John, "I'm sure you know the Bible well enough to explain it to him."

He replied, "But there's no link from my brain to his to transfer the information. How can I get it across to him in a systematic, organized manner? That's why we need these books."

She sighed, "Well, whatever you want to do."

They wanted to please each other. Then he wavered and said, "I'm sorry. Thank you for coming, but I'm sorry; we can't do it."

The thought flashed into my mind to offer a discounted set we had at home, and they accepted. So, we shipped them the books and let them know a lot of people were praying for them and their son. A few months later they had paid off their books, and we received the following letter from John:

Re: Gabe,

I wanted to write and thank you for all the prayers and well wishes that you have sent our way for Gabe. It means a lot to us that you have done that and we hope that we can return the favor if needed (we hope that you never need our prayers as badly as we did yours). I also wanted to share news with you of our recent cardiology check up with Gabe.

In August, Gabe's regular cardiologist referred us to go to Eggleston Hospital (EH) for another valvuplasty, citing the pressure in his chest as being a gradient of 70. The physicians at EH agreed with that doctor upon examination of his file. At EH, they were to perform a catheter first to verify the non-invasive gradient readings.

They returned Gabe to us after he had only been gone an hour and told us that the catheter found a pressure of only 40 and that he did not need a valvuplasty! They told us that it seemed that he may be an aortic patient that never needs another intervention; the valvuplasty that he had at four months of age may last him for a lifetime. That would be a wait and (pray) see kind of thing, though.

God does answer prayers! Thank you so much for yours on our behalf!

Sincerely,

John C.

We praise God that He does hear and answer prayers for our customers—and sometimes He lets us in on the answers!

Chapter 27

Already on Our List

Jennie's house stood in a big field with a few buildings full of heavy-duty equipment out back. As we drove up the long drive, we counted five dogs of various sizes. Larry handed me the e-mail request for *The Bible Story* and said, "This one is yours, dearie."

I laughed. I knew it was mine. I am the official dog tester on our team. The mongrels were friendly enough, and three extra hound pups came gamboling toward us as we walked to the porch. Another dog began barking inside when we knocked. Jennie squeezed out the door when she heard why we had come. Her nine-year-old daughter followed her.

She apologized for all the furniture and equipment stacked on the porch and then said, "But could you show me the books right here? We've just pulled up all the carpet, and we're redoing the floor, so it's really bad inside." She said they had bought the old farmhouse and paid it off quickly. Now they were finally able to go on with renovations without a big mortgage over their heads.

> *Jennie told us she was not raised in church, and she had almost no knowledge of the Bible. She was hungry to learn more.*

Jennie told us she was not raised in church, and she had almost no knowledge of the Bible. She was hungry to learn more. She said, "I thought if I started on this level with my children, I could learn too."

As we stood there, paging through the books on top of a stack of used furniture, I could feel the three hound puppies playfully biting and tugging the edge of my skirt. I ignored them as Jennie leaned over the books, intensely interested.

Jennie said that she and her husband have their own business, laying underground cable at construction sites. She was happy to put down her deposit for *The Bible Story, Bible Readings,* and *Triumph of God's Love.* As we packed up the books to leave, Jennie asked, "Don't you think God does things for people sometimes just to encourage them personally?"

"Yes," I replied. "And God put you on our schedule before you sent in your e-mail. The first week of January I took one day and struggled all day to work out our general schedule for the year since we work in such a wide area. Then the last week of January an angel must have nudged you and said, 'It's time to send that e-mail for *The Bible Story.*'"

As we left, Jennie's face was still glowing. We all knew that we had come to her house that day because God had already put her on our list.

Chapter 28

Dog-Eared Books

The day was hot, and we stopped at the city library to refresh ourselves. Larry went into the children's section to look for some of our books. What he found was a few worn out, dog-eared copies of *My Bible Friends* in the old, two-story-per-book format. The books looked over thirty years old with hard usage. Larry asked to speak with the purchasing agent of the library. He was told that she had gone out for a couple of hours but would be back from 6:00 to 8:00 p.m. to help close down.

When we came back that evening, we took in a few books in our shoulder bag. Tasha, the director, was waiting for us. I brought her a couple of the dog-eared *My Bible Friends* off the shelf, and Larry held out the gleaming new one, saying, "Here's what they look like now," and began laying our books on the counter. She was immediately interested, and in a moment, Larry brought in our two briefcases of display books.

As Tasha looked at set after set of our books, she was impressed. She asked, "Could you give me the prices so I can figure out which sets I can take this time?"

She began stacking the books she liked best in a pile. *My Bible Friends* and the *Encyclopedia of Foods and Their Healing Power* went first, then *Great Stories for Kids*. She thumbed through the book called *Jacob* from the new *Family Bible Stories*, and said, "These are really nice," and added it to the stack. With the *Bible Reference Library*, she liked the references and indexes; then she held up *The Desire of Ages* and pointed to the spine of the book. "That's really beautiful," she said, "I'd like to read that." I hadn't given much thought to the importance of eye appeal on a book spine before, but that is how one sees most of the books at the library.

As Larry wrote up the order for these five sets that she chose, Tasha said, "This is a small library—just a two-man operation. When my partner comes in tomorrow, I'll tell her I just ordered $1,000 worth of books."

Then she added, "It was really nice to handle the actual books. I don't usually get to do that when I order. When you come next year, maybe I can get some of them in the Spanish editions."

We left, praising God for letting us have the privilege of putting our books where they will be used and appreciated, and for letting us replace some old, dog-eared books!

Chapter 29

Twice Adopted

Pastor Jerry invited me into his home so he could look at *The Bible Story* and other books for his church. As we talked about the issues young people are facing today, I realized that this man was sincerely interested in the youth of his church. He told me that he had been pastoring for six years now after retiring from other work, and he just loved it. He thought some of our books would be a real blessing in his ministry, and soon I had samples of *The Bible Story, Bible Reference Library, My Bible Friends,* and *Bedtime Stories* spread across the floor.

He said his adopted eleven-year-old son was at school today, but his three grandchildren from out of town were in the back room playing video games. "I can hardly get them to go outside and play because they are so attached to the games!" he added.

Pastor Jerry said he thought *The Bible Story* would be a real teaching tool for the children at home and a resource for teachers at his church. He was especially moved as we looked through the *Bible Readings*.

When it was time to order, he said, "I think it would be better if I get the books and use them from my home. If I just get them and leave them at the church, the teachers may not appreciate them, and they might just

> *With my contract pad in my lap, I reached into my case for Great Stories for Kids and said, "I think this set would be just what your son needs. It deals with so many issues kids are facing today—adoption, bullies, abuse, drugs, guns, getting along with others."*

sit on the shelf." He pondered the cost and his budget and apologized that he could not order everything today. "I'll get my daughter to order *The Bible Story*," he said. "But I really want something to help my son."

Pastor Jerry said they had adopted him a year ago. Then he shared this story: The boy had been placed in foster care in the tragic aftermath of parental drug use and irresponsibility. He had been shuffled from home to home as he grew up and finally ended up in a boys' home. "You know the older they get, the harder it is for them to be adopted," he said.

When he was about ten, a man from a large city came and chose Daniel and took him to his new home. The new dad had been told about Daniel's learning problems and emotional baggage from his past. But the man was sure everything would work out, and he went ahead with the adoption. One month later he called the boys' home and said he was bringing Daniel back. The adoption was off.

At this point the Department of Family and Children's Services called Pastor Jerry and his wife who had fostered several children over the years. They told him about Daniel and pleaded, "You just have to take him. We sent him away with a big adoption, good-bye party and it will break his heart to go back to the boys' home. Please, you've got to take him!"

So, they did. "And we just fell in love with him!" Pastor Jerry finished.

With my contract pad in my lap, I reached into my case for *Great Stories for Kids* and said, "I think this set would be just what your son needs. It deals with so many issues kids are facing today—adoption, bullies, abuse, drugs, guns, getting along with others."

He reached for the book and paged through it. "Yes! I think these would help my son," he said. "And I really want this one too," he added as he picked up the *Bible Readings* again.

When I left, I was praising God that He had provided again for this special son who was twice adopted.

Chapter 30

In Spite of Opposition

I had been to Nadine's neighborhood before and found her house, but she was not home. It was a working-class neighborhood, not terribly prosperous, not terribly poor, and there was evidence of children in the home. Her card was for the *Family Medical Guide*. Later my trainer was working with me, and we went to find Nadine.

When my supervisor and I knocked, both she and her husband were doing the dishes. The three children were getting ready for bed. They invited us into a much-cluttered kitchen. Nadine cleared enough of the table so we could set the books on it, and then invited us to sit down. (I was glad the books had washable Mylar covers!)

Her husband was friendly at the beginning. He jokingly said that he washed the dishes sometimes for his wife because it helped get his fingernails clean. We invited him to look at the books with us. But he said, "No, I'm not interested in that." He took his mug of beer and went into the other room to watch TV. So, we proceeded with the demonstration.

Nadine sat down at the table with us, and the children came to look. They were all less than eight years old. Between puffs on her cigarette, Nadine told us that the main reason she wanted the books was that they had so much sickness in their home. It seemed like she was always going to the doctor's office. If she took one child, she had to take all three. Even though her sister and mother are both nurses, and they often help her, there are times when nobody knows what to do, so she ends up in the emergency room or the doctor's office. She thought there ought to be better answers than that.

She was very pleased as she looked through the medical books and found them to be very useful and in everyday language. The children were curious but polite, and from time to time she paused to ask them if they were getting ready for bed with the pajamas on, teeth brushed, and so on.

When we presented the *Bible Readings for the Home*, she became more interested and said that she felt this would help her have answers for the children and herself.

Her spouse came back into the kitchen just in time to hear the price, and the fight was on. He began to oppose her, and she began to resist him. During the details of the payment plan, down payment, and so on, the man paced back and forth from the living room to the kitchen, getting louder and louder with his profanity and objections. He stormed, "How do you think we're going to eat? We can't eat books!"

Nadine turned to one of her children and said, "Bring me my purse."

He said, "What?! You're putting a down payment on that? Don't put my name on it!"

She replied, "Don't worry about it. I'm taking responsibility for this."

He was very angry. He finished up collecting the garbage and took the huge bag of trash outside. In the moment that he was outside, Nadine said to us, "My address is going to change this weekend, but he doesn't know that yet."

Her little girl said, "Oh, yes! Shhhh!"

Then he came back into the room. Nadine got out her checkbook for the down payment. Again, her husband razzed her about the order, and she retorted, "The tax refund is coming, and I'll take my half, thank you!"

Then very calmly she turned to the children and said, "Have you brushed your teeth yet? You need to get ready for bed."

It was amazing to see the conflict going on, and yet the calmness with which she handled her children. Even the husband, in talking to the children, did not include them in the fight.

As she wrote her check, he razzed her one more time, and I saw her write fiercely, "Forty-five," on the check and then with a very strong motion, she slashed the line across and put zero-zero over 100. She was determined to have the books.

We offered her the Bible course, and she said, "Yes." We had prayer with her before we left. I was afraid that she might cancel, or that her credit approval would not go through. But as the days passed, the reports came back, and my pay came in. I was very pleased to know, at least this far, that the order was saved. I kept her in my prayers.

A few months later the office asked me to check and make sure her statements were getting through to her. I went and found that she had indeed followed through on her move to a different location. She told me that she had gone back several times to make sure that when UPS delivered the books, she could pick up her package before her husband got off work because he had threatened that if he found them, he would tear them up and throw them away.

She had successfully intercepted the package and started using the books. She was very happy as she answered her little boy's questions about the Bible from her books. She also said things were getting better with her husband after he had started getting help about his drinking. I prayed with her again and praised God for helping her to be faithful in spite of opposition.

Chapter 31

These Dogs Bite!

When Larry pulled into the yard at Glenda's, there were five or six dogs lying around. But none of them got up to bark. They just watched the car. He wasn't sure whether to get out or not. Then the door of the house opened, and a young man came out. Larry lowered his window as the man approached the car and asked, "Who are you looking for?"

He held out the medical lead card and asked, "Is Glenda home?"

The man replied, "Yes, but she's not feeling well at this time."

Handing over the card, Larry asked him to go see if she was feeling well enough to look at these. The man took it and disappeared into the house. In a few minutes Glenda came out, and Larry questioned her about the card as she came around to the driver's side. As he was about to get out, he asked, "Do you think your dogs will bite?"

"Yes, I know they will," she replied.

Quickly he pulled his leg back into the car as a dog's head appeared below the door. Then all the dogs burst out barking. After quieting the dogs, Glenda came back to the passenger side and leaned in the window. A little, short lady, she said she had worked at the local state mental hospital for many years. Larry proceeded to canvass her from the inside of the car while she stood outside.

> *She said she would use her birthday money to get these beautiful books.*

He showed her a little in the *Family Medical Guide* books, and when he pulled out *The Desire of Ages*, her eyes lit up. After reading some passages from it, she said, "That was so beautiful the way you read that. It was like you were right there."

They had fellowship in the Lord as she was hanging into the car window. When he told her the cost of the books and how she could get them, she mentioned that the day before was her birthday, and someone had given her cash. She said she would use her birthday money to get these beautiful books.

While finishing the paperwork, she disclosed a number of health conditions that she has had and that it is a miracle that she is even alive today. She has undergone a heart transplant and also lives with lupus and epilepsy. She was just coming out of another grand mal seizure when Larry came to show her the books. What a precious lady! Please pray for Glenda.

Chapter 32

The Wood Stove Order

When we met Rick, he was fixing his John Deere equipment. He had sent in a lead card inquiring about our *Foods* encyclopedias. He told us that he had gone through a valve replacement in his heart. He put everything down and came inside to look at the books with his wife Dee. They liked the books, but his medical overhead had put them under tremendous financial strain. They were preparing their house for sale to lift the burden.

As I spread out the books, Larry saw a wood stove in their extra family room/kitchen. He asked if he could look at it. He really became interested in it. They told us they didn't really use it much. As I finished showing the books, Rick said, "I'm sorry. These are really nice, but we really can't do anything right now. We are just strapped financially." I offered our little five-book set of paperbacks for twenty dollars and he chose to get them. He handed me the twenty dollars, and his wife Dee accepted a tract on how to stop smoking.

We were all standing around the work island in the active kitchen. Larry stepped up and asked if they were serious about selling the wood stove. The man said yes and named a reasonable price. It was close to the price of the books. Larry said, "Maybe we could trade. Will you be here next Sunday so we could come and get it?" Rick said he would have it disconnected and ready to go.

After we left, we discussed with each other the trading of our demonstrator set of *Foods and Their Healing Power* for the stove. We couldn't let the books go that day because it was Monday, and we still needed them for the week's work. We had another set at home, but we would not be there again until Friday. We called Rick and Dee back, and they agreed to the trade.

When we finished our work for the night, we drove back to our camper. We were parked at a church member's house for that one night before going farther south. We stopped in to tell her about our day's adventures, including the excitement over the wood stove. Carrie was excited with us. Then she said, "You know, there's a set of books that I looked at when I ate at your house one Sabbath. But I usually only see you on Sabbaths, and we don't do business then. I'd like to see those books again. They were health books."

"Oh, Carrie, those were the *Foods* books," I said.

She replied, "I'd like to look at them again. Since God has given me this good job, I'm ready to get them now." So, the Lord gave us an order for that set of books that night after all.

The next Sunday Larry and my dad drove back to Rick's house to deliver their books and pick up the stove. He told me it took four men and a dog to load it onto our trailer. It was heavy! But it is a good stove, and now as we sit by the fire, we thank the Lord for it and for what He did—putting orders for our health books into two homes on the same day when He gave us the wood stove order.

Chapter 33

Entertaining Angels

We never know how we'll be received when we knock, but I'm sure angels smile, too, at some of the responses we get. When we walked up to Adam's door, he held up both hands and said, "I didn't do it! I don't want any!"

I held the *Encyclopedia of Foods* lead card up for him to see, and he had to admit it was his own handwriting. But he tried to put us off, saying he didn't have the time, he was about to go somewhere, and he didn't want an interview! I opened the sample book and started paging through it, asking if he'd seen something that piqued his interest in the doctor's office. He glanced through the pages and finally said, "Oh, come on in!"

In a few minutes he was looking at the full-sized volumes of the books and having a lively chat with Larry about experiences in the military. As he wrote a check for the full amount, his only question was, "How soon will I get all of these?"

At Janine's home, we found her very interested in the *Foods* books, and her husband Greg, very interested in entertaining us while we talked. He proudly described some of his hunting trips, pointing to two mounted deer heads and a huge boar's head on the wall. He told us he is sixty-seven and still working full-time in the maintenance department of the county high school. As Larry shared a few features about the books, Greg interrupted again and again with tricks—cards, coins, and his dog's trick performance.

Janine spoke up at one point and told him he better listen up since he was the one that was going to pay for the books. She really wanted them. She told me, on the side, that if he eats any meat, she bakes it for him rather than frying. In the middle of all their birds, cats, and dogs, she was doing all she could to protect his health.

After an hour of entertainment, Greg signed his deposit on *The Desire of Ages, Family Medical Guide,* and our *Encyclopedia of Foods* books. He removed his cap and bowed for prayer, then proudly led Larry back to his hobby room to show him his collection of guns, pocketknives, and coins. We got home late that night, thankful for what God had done, and certain that we and our angels had been thoroughly entertained!

Chapter 34

A Woman, a Dream, and a "*Happy D*"

Margie's e-mail was for info on *God Cares/Daniel and Revelation*. She exclaimed, "You mean you came all the way from Dublin to find me?" as she invited us in. Margie and Jim were watching the aftermath of Hurricane Katrina on TV. We invited Jim to sit closer where he could see the books, but he said, "I'm not really interested. She's the one that wants them."

Larry showed the *God Cares/Daniel and Revelation* books to Margie. She wanted something understandable for teaching Sunday school.

She asked, "Do you have something that takes you through the whole Bible?"

"As a matter of fact, I do," Larry replied. "Here's our *Bible Reference Library* for adults." He spread out our accordion folder and began telling her about each book. Margie was delighted.

"You have it all!" she exclaimed. "It's a whole library! Now I won't have to go hunting for a book here and a book there when I'm teaching. I can get all the help I need right here."

Then she told us how she began teaching adults. She said about eight months ago she dreamed she was at church, and the pastor had called her up to the pulpit and was handing over some papers and things for her to take over his Sunday school class. When she woke up, she said, "Lord, I don't do adults. Kids are my thing. I don't know what this is all about."

She stuffed the dream aside and forgot about it. Then in July the pastor announced that the first Sunday in August he would be starting up a youth class. He said, "Be thinking it over because one of you needs to teach this class."

Margie thought, "I hope someone volunteers. We need a teacher."

A couple of weeks later the pastor said again, "I need someone to teach this class. Next week is my last one."

A woman beside Margie looked at her and said, "Margie, I think you should teach this class. You would be good at it."

Margie was shocked. "Who me?" she said. Then she remembered the dream.

When she looked up, the pastor said, "Margie, could you stay for a moment after class?"

So, she did. When he started to speak to her, he said, "Don't worry, I'm not asking you to take the class."

But Margie replied, "Let me tell you something. I believe God has laid it on my heart to teach this class."

The pastor said, "Praise the Lord! Never mind what I was going to ask you to do. It can wait."

"So," Margie finished, "I'm just up to my fourth Sunday teaching, and these books will be wonderful. How much are they?"

When Larry gave the price, Margie exclaimed, "Is that all?!"

She turned to Jim and asked, "What do you think, dear?"

He said, "It's up to you. Will you use them?"

"Oh, yes," she said, "I will really use these. I really want them!"

"Then go ahead," he answered.

I looked in my bag for a *Happiness Digest* to leave with Margie, but I didn't have one. I decided to go out to the Blazer and get her one in English and one in Spanish since she had told us about the outreach her church has to the Spanish migrant workers in the area. When I came back in with that pink book in my hand, Margie cried out, "Oh, there's my book!"

She reached for it eagerly. She said, "The week before my first class, I was thinking about what I should teach and looking through all my books, but I couldn't settle on anything. I got all the way to Thursday, and I was asking God what to do. I took my car in for an oil change—it was a month overdue. There in the invoice basket on the counter I saw this book, *Happiness Digest*. I asked the clerk where she got it."

> *After we prayed with them, Margie said, "I want you to know without a doubt God sent you here this very day!" Indeed, He had. We marveled as we drove away.*

The clerk said that a young person from out of state had come in, raising money for their college expenses, and she had given a donation for the book. Margie borrowed it and leafed back and forth in it while her car was being serviced. Then she saw the chapter, "You Can If You Will," and her attention was riveted. She asked the clerk to run her a copy of that chapter, and she took it and taught from it for her first Sunday school class. "It's about obedience," she added. "And now I get to have my own copy!" She hugged the little book. She was ecstatic.

After we prayed with them, Margie said, "I want you to know without a doubt God sent you here this very day!" Indeed, He had. We marveled as we drove away.

Chapter 35

When We Meet Again

We're always happy to meet our customers the first time and help them make an order. But when we meet again, and they order again, it's an extra thrill.

We met Margie and Jim back in 2005 on the day after Hurricane Katrina hit the Gulf Coast. At that time, Margie was glad to order the *Daniel and Revelation/God Cares* books and the *Bible Reference Library*. She was especially excited to receive her own copy of the *Happiness Digest*. She had found a copy at an oil change garage and procured copies of a chapter for teaching her first adult Sunday school class.

We met them again this week when we ran a lead on their country road. The lead was not really interested, so I said to Larry, "Let's go see Margie."

Jim opened the door and invited us in, and Margie stood up from her seat in the kitchen and exclaimed, "The Bazemore's! Come in! How are you? I remembered your name!"

They invited us to come on in and sit down in the living room and visit. After listening for a few minutes, I held out our display book of the *Encyclopedia of Foods and Their Healing Power*.

Margie took the book, exclaiming, "This is so amazing! My sister and I have really been getting into this lately and praying about our responsibility to God for our health." She said she thinks most of our problems come from a lack of self-control. Pointing to her mouth, she added, "I think most of it starts right here."

> *I thought of our first visit four years before when Jim sat across the room, stoically disinterested. Now he sat a few feet away, participating.*

I asked Larry to go bring me our health case, and in a moment Margie and Jim were both looking at our books. I thought of our first visit four years before when Jim sat across the room, stoically disinterested. Now he sat a few feet away, participating. He was not quite close enough to see well, so I handed him volume 2 until I needed it to show Margie.

He sat, turning pages, while Margie and I talked and went through volume 1. Jim exclaimed, "We eat all this stuff!"

Margie said her blood pressure was high, so she was very interested. She asked, "Do you go by this? Is it hard to set up your kitchen this way? How long does it take?"

I said I was raised this way. The only big change I made was when I learned how to cook without dairy and eggs, and we quit buying them. We're always trying to do better as we learn more. I assured her that the transition recipes and healthy kitchen section in volume 3 would be a real help, and that it's not hard.

Margie said to Jim, "I really want these! You know I love books!"

She decided to take *Health Power* for cash today and put down her deposit on an order for the *Foods* books. We prayed together and I pulled out a *Christ's Object Lessons* to leave as a gift book, saying, "I know we left you *Happiness Digest* last time, so here's a different one today."

At the mention of the *Happiness Digest*, Margie bubbled over, "Oh, yes! I used it for teaching my class, and I ordered a whole case so everybody could have one, and they just loved it!"

We never know how God will multiply our efforts! I pray that we will see Margie and Jim and their whole flock in heaven one day when we meet again!

PART II

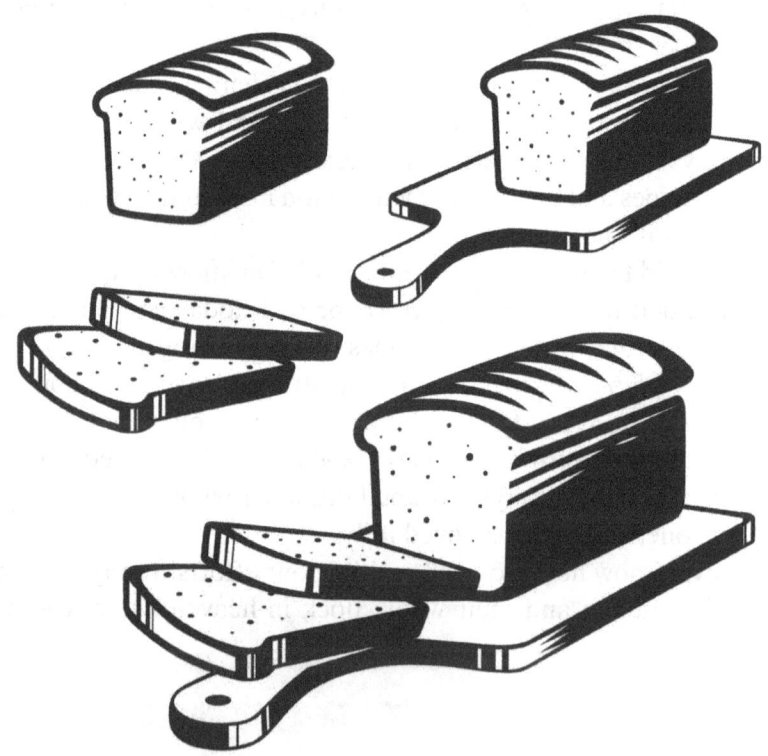

SLICES & CRUMBS
Small Books & Free Literature

Please note: Names in the following stories have been changed to protect the identity of our clients.

Chapter 1

The Value of Crumbs

In our work of bringing literature to the people, I often refer to a set of books as a loaf, small books for $5 or $10 as slices, and free literature as crumbs. After all, the Bread of Life is present in all of our literature, and it is our job to bring Him to the people. I carry a box in our vehicle, containing the leftovers from church—*Our Little Friend, Primary Treasures,* etc.—as well as leftovers from our work—worn-out copies of *The Bible Story* from doctors' offices. I pass these out freely in the homes of the poor and the laundromats where they frequently go. The promise is that God's word will not come back to Him void, so I go on casting out crumbs as well as loaves and slices.

We were running leads in a small town when I came to Granny's house. She had sent in a card for information on *The Bible Story, Bible Reference Library*, and *Family Bible*. As I walked through the cluttered dirt of the yard, I could tell that a lot of people lived in the house. Inside I found Granny seated at the far end of the room with several grown children, grandchildren, and babies gathered around. She invited me to sit by her and show her the books.

As she told me some of the details of their survival, I knew they were in very tight financial straits, so I pulled out the little set of five—the *Bible Readings, The Desire of Ages, The Ministry of Healing, Christ's Object Lessons,* and *The Great Controversy*. The children crowded around, eager to see what Granny was getting. She said, "These are nice. I'll take these," and dug into her purse for twenty dollars.

I said, "I have something nice out in the vehicle for the children," and went out for a handful of our church literature.

When she took the papers, she handed out the *Our Little Friends* to the kids, but at the bottom of the stack were three *Primary Treasure*

Quarterlies. The children reached eagerly for them, but Granny hugged them to herself.

"Oh, no," she said. "We are saving these so we can have something nice in Sunday school!"

I walked back to our vehicle with a lump in my throat. They had so little, and we have so much. From the discarded leftovers from my own little home church, they had recognized the value of the crumbs.

Even the Fragments are Precious—

We should treat as a sacred treasure every line of printed matter containing present truth. Even the fragments of a pamphlet or of a periodical should be regarded as of value. Who can estimate the influence that a torn page containing the truths of the third angel's message may have upon the heart of some seeker after truth? Let us remember that somebody would be glad to read all the books and papers we can spare. Every page is a ray of light from heaven, to shine into the highways and the hedges, shedding light upon the pathway of truth.[2]

---

[2] Ellen G. White, *Colporteur Ministry* (Mountain View, CA: Pacific Press, 1953), p. 151, emphasis mine.

Chapter 2

Answers for Her Questions

Kim left her neighbor at the picnic table and walked us down to her little apartment. The tiny space around her door was filled with cantaloupe vines, and yellow gladiolas bloomed in a window box. Bright red salvia lined the wall over to the tiny patio where tomatoes were ripening on the vines in their big, blue pots. Indoors, the apartment was orderly and clean.

Kim said she had sent in *The Bible Story* card for herself because she enjoyed the book so much in the doctor's office. She said, "I read the Bible, but I'm not sure I always get the meaning. These really help."

As I showed her volume 1, Kim asked, "How could Lucifer rebel against God right in heaven?! I just can't understand that!"

I said, "The Bible calls it the mystery of iniquity. Just think, with all the results of evil around us, and knowing the consequences, why do we go ahead and sin?"

"But he was in heaven!" she said.

So, we talked about the power of choice God gave us and how He wants obedience from love. I read about Adam and Eve in Eden and how they failed in the story, "The Test of Love," and about God's promise of a Redeemer in "One Gleam of Hope."

As she went for her Bible on the Noah story, she said, "Well, I don't believe in 'once saved, always saved.' I don't think the Bible teaches that. I've known people who were saved, and then they backslid."

Larry spoke up, "Satan was once saved, but he is not saved now."

Kim was full of questions, and I read more to her from the books than I usually do. She had told us that her son had been murdered, and she had moved to Georgia to get away from a bad relationship herself and to make a new start in life. She wanted more answers about what happens at death, so I read her the whole story in volume 10, explaining 1 Thessalonians 4 about the dead who are asleep in Jesus and resurrected at His coming. I paused on the page showing Jesus coming and people coming out of their graves. Kim looked up and exclaimed, "This gives me hope!"

She loved the books but couldn't order today. When I showed her the little sample of *The Bible Story* and our set of five small books, she was interested. She fished in her pocket for money, saying, "I have $13, and I need $6 for a co-pay at the clinic this afternoon."

"Would you like to give $7 and trade some tomatoes for these books?" I asked.

"Sure! Do I get this one too?" she asked, reaching for the little sample of *The Bible Story*.

I nodded. "I can't wait to start reading," she smiled. "These are my first tomatoes," she added. "Now I know why I didn't pick them yesterday—it was a God thing—so I'd have them for you!"

It was indeed "a God thing" so Kim could get answers for her questions!

Chapter 3

Jump Out and Run!

We were heading to our last lead at the end of a burning hot day when Larry suddenly swung our Blazer into a corner convenience store parking lot, exclaiming, "They need help!"

Leaving our engine running, he jumped out and ran toward two men who were pushing a heavily loaded pickup truck uphill to the gas pumps. As I perceived what was going on, I decided my few pounds of push might make a difference.

I snatched the key from our ignition and dropped it under the floor mat, then ran to join the men as they struggled to keep the truck from rolling back downhill. We would all heave, then the driver would jump in and slam on the brake as the truck began to drift backward.

We inched forward, trying to get the vehicle onto the level pad in reach of the gas pump. Sweat drenched, we caught our breath for a moment until the driver called, "Ready?" Suddenly another pickup swung into the lot and a tall man jumped out and came running to my corner. I let go and stepped back as he helped heave the truck on up to the pumps. The driver jumped out with profuse thanks to us all as the big man walked back to his truck and drove off.

The driver whipped out his wallet and pulled out twenty dollars to thank us.

The driver whipped out his wallet and pulled out twenty dollars to thank us. Larry held up his hands in protest, saying, "We were just helping you."

The man held the twenty dollars toward me, and I saw my opportunity for literature. I reached for the money with a slight, courteous bow and said, "Let me give you something in exchange for this."

Then I ran to our Blazer and grabbed a set of our little books—*The Great Controversy, The Ministry of Healing, Christ's Object Lessons, The Desire of Ages,* and *Bible Readings*. I hurried back to the driver, holding out the books. His young face glowed through the streaming sweat as he took the set, saying, "This is my blessing today!"

A few days later we finished up a demo of *The Bible Story* for a woman who had lost most of a leg when she was run over by a reckless motorcyclist. Her life had greatly changed after the accident, and she found it a real struggle to resist depression and discouragement. She had found some hope in our books but was unable to order today or even to give five dollars for a small book.

When Larry asked if the family would like to trade something for the small set of books, Grandma went to the kitchen and began digging in the cupboards for supplies—canned goods and a new bottle of oil—to exchange for the books.

We were driving away on their dirt road when Larry exclaimed, "There's a snake!"

It was a large, poisonous one, so he ran over it and then backed up to deal with it. The injured snake was weaving its way across the ditch. Larry jumped out and seized a dead tree branch for a weapon. He dragged the snake back onto the road and killed it. When he got back in, I asked, "How's your adrenaline level?"

"Up!" he laughed. Then he added, "When I see poisonous snakes on the road where kids are running around, I try to do something about it."

I agreed. And that's really what we're trying to do, fighting that old serpent, the devil, as we go from home to home. We just never know when we may need to jump out and run!

Chapter 4

Jason's Goals

As Ernest walked out to meet us with his little two-year-old daughter Lila, I said to Larry, "That man's back hurts."

As we spoke, he said, "Yes, after five operations it still hurts."

His wife Diane came out. She had sent *The Bible Story* card in. I asked if Lila was their only child. She said, "Yes—our miracle baby. Our son was killed in an accident in 2000."

She said they had been told they could never have any more children, but God gave them Lila and they wanted to get *The Bible Story* for her.

Diane invited us to sit down in the screened-in porch. Before Larry could open his case to show the books, she said, "Let me share something with you." She went back inside and brought out a framed art project. She explained, "Jason was twelve when he died. He was run over by a school bus on his way home from school. It was the day after Martin Luther King, Jr. Day in 2000. Two days after the funeral his friends brought us this."

The friends told Ernest and Diane that on the day Jonathan died his teacher had shared with the children about Martin Luther King, Jr. and his famous words, "I have a dream." She had challenged the children to make a poster showing their dreams and goals.

Jason had written his goals on four white clouds. The first one was, "That I could bring 100 people to Christ." The others were about helping people to get along and not to fight each other.

Diane said, "Jason had already given his heart to Jesus. He actually wrote these goals not many minutes before he died. We have shared this on the Internet and have received back hundreds of responses. We are so glad we have this." What a consolation God gave them for the death of their child!

Then Larry presented *The Bible Story* and *Bible Readings*, but they were not able to order yet. So, Larry shared our small set of five paperbacks, including *The Great Controversy* and *The Desire of Ages*. Ernest was very interested. He has had a hard time reconciling the hypocrisy and wealth of many professed, televised Christians with the crying needs of humanity.

Ernest said, "I want these. I'll read them."

When we offered to pray before we left, Ernest knelt, saying, "I just feel better on my knees." We all knelt together as Larry prayed for them. Please remember Ernest's family in your prayers. Remember, Jesus said, "I am the good shepherd, and know my sheep, and am known of mine" (John 10:14).

CHAPTER 5

Someone Special Behind the Door

It was the day before Christmas, and we were knocking spontaneously on doors to finish our week. When we knocked at the first house a voice called out, "Come in!"

I pushed the door open cautiously and called out, "Hello!"

The room was semi-dark, and an elderly woman was sitting at the dining room table. It was an orderly room with a few red bows and Christmas ornaments displayed. The lady laughed when she saw us and said she thought we were somebody else. I invited her to do our survey, but after question number one, she was not satisfied until she knew our names and had *The Bible Story* flyer in her hand to know who we were. Then she was glad to do the four other questions.

Her middle-aged son, visiting from New York City, stood by. Karen appreciated what we were doing, and when I presented our set of little books, she became very interested. As her son went to bring her purse, she told us she studies a lot, teaches Sunday school, and has her own Bible study group on Friday nights there in her home. She said she is trying to tell everyone she can about Jesus.

"These will be a real help," she said as she took the set and thumbed through the books again. I'm sure God will multiply the Bread of Life at Karen's table.

Further down the street, we met a grandmother who had adopted her five-year-old grandson. "So, now I'm his mom," she said with a smile. She took *My Friend Jesus* and *Prince of Peace*.

Several people later we met Michael. As we walked into the carport, we wondered if anyone was home besides the big gray cat. A fishing boat dominated the space and a variety of vehicles and other equipment sat in the yard.

After Larry knocked twice, Michael stepped out to greet us. He was neatly dressed in his fisherman's cap, plaid flannel shirt, jeans, and new, heavy-duty boots. As we talked, he said he wished he could get *The Bible Story* but money was a problem right now. He said, "This would be a help to my son."

Larry asked, "How old is he?"

"Oh, he's twenty. He and his wife are youth ministers at his church," Michael replied.

"Twenty!" Larry exclaimed. "You don't look old enough to have a son that's twenty!"

"Well, I'm thirty-seven," Michael replied. "When I was twenty, my wife and I were youth ministers."

But Michael had had some hard times. After fourteen years that marriage had ended in divorce. Then he married again, but that one wasn't meant to be, he said. "Now I'm raising a five-year-old daughter alone," he finished.

When we showed our little books, Michael said, "I need to read the Bible more."

He looked back and forth at the titles and paged through the books. Finally, he chose *Christ's Object Lessons* and *The Ministry of Healing*. He gladly accepted Larry's offer to pray for him before we left.

Until we knock, we never know what joy or sorrow we'll meet, but we always know that there is someone special behind the door!

Chapter 6

Shocking News

By the time we reached the trailer park on Sugar Sand Road, it was dark and the lot numbers were very hard to find. Larry pulled into a driveway where we saw some people with an outside light on. I waited in the car while he took the lead card to go ask for help. I could see the two young Hispanic men gesturing and talking to Larry as well as scolding their big hound which was jumping around their feet. In a moment, Larry came back and said, "Come on. This isn't the place but they want to look."

As we climbed the shaky, wooden steps into the single-wide trailer, I realized we were entering a multifamily, Catholic background, Spanish culture home. Juan called his wife Selena to come to the kitchen table and she came with the baby in her arms. They knew limited English and we knew even less Spanish, but we did have *The Bible Story* volume 1 and *Bible Readings* in Spanish. They leaned forward with interest as Larry talked and turned the pages. When he came to the picture of Jesus' second coming in the *Bible Readings*, he said, "The whole purpose of the library is to help families get ready for this. I don't know about you folks, but I believe that Jesus is coming back soon."

The young mother looked up from the picture with an expression of total shock on her face. "Really?!" she blurted out. She reached for the book and stared at the pages as if she had never before heard that Jesus is coming back, let alone soon! She told her husband, "We need this book." But they were unable to order the set. Larry said, "I have one paperback copy of *Bible Readings* in Spanish out in the car. You can have that for five dollars. Would you like that?"

"Oh, yes!" Juan said. "We can give five dollars tonight."

Selena kept looking at the picture and the questions and Bible verses while I went out to get the thick little book in their language. We prayed with them before we left.

A few days later Larry said to me, "Remember that Spanish couple that got the *Bible Readings*? That really was a divine appointment. That was in the wrong trailer park on Sugar Sand Road." Praise God! He knows where the right people are!

CHAPTER 7

Death Sentence Faith

Our visit with David and his family was refreshing. After showing books to several families who were apparently able to spend money but unwilling to order or even to donate for one small book, we came to David's house. He had sent in a card about our *Foods and Their Healing Power* books.

The living room was small, and David leaned back in his recliner with a couple days' growth of beard on his face. An empty wheelchair was just a step away and other furniture crowded the edges of the small room. David invited me to sit down in the wheelchair as he talked. He introduced Larry and me to his faithful wife and attentive teenage daughter. He explained how the *Foods* book had caught his attention in a doctor's office.

He said, "I have bone cancer." The doctors really couldn't do a lot more for him and had pretty much sent him home with a death sentence. But David's face was calm as he told us he knew a better Physician, and that he trusted his care to Him. He looked upward and smiled. That was why he was interested in all the natural foods he saw in the book.

I shared some of the materials from volumes 1 and 2, wondering how much to say. It was at least a week until the end of the month and no one in the family was employed. I could see open boxes scattered on the table and floor behind David and his wife, so I decided to ask a few more questions about their lives. "It looks like you're getting ready to move," I ventured.

David replied, "Yes, I've made arrangements for my family to be cared for and have a house for them to live in that belongs to a friend of ours." He indicated a city about thirty miles away where he goes to the doctor. I asked if anything would keep him from ordering today.

"Just money," he smiled.

I pulled out our little softback set—*The Ministry of Healing, The Desire of Ages, The Great Controversy, Patriarchs and Prophets,* and *Bible*

Readings—and made our standard offer: $5 each or $20 for the set. His eyes lighted up as he reached for the books. His wife leaned over, and they held a muffled powwow.

"Do you have any money?" she whispered.

"Yes, I still have the laundry money," he whispered back.

Then he said joyfully to me, "I'll take these and don't worry—they will be used!"

He fished his twenty-dollar bill out of his coveralls pocket and held it out to me. Then we joined hands in a circle and prayed for David and his family, certain that God would bless this man in his death sentence faith!

Chapter 8

A Little Angel, Beer Cans, or Vidalia Onions

The backyard looked like there had been a recent fire. Charred remains of clutter and a burned-out trampoline caught my eye. As I knocked at the back door, a voice inside demanded, "Who is it?"

In my least threatening voice I called out, "It's Gladys Joy! Is Kelsey here?"

When the door opened, Kelsey and a friend stood there. I held out *The Bible Story* lead card and explained why I was there. Kelsey apologized for her rudeness and told me she was fearful because she has a stalker interfering with her life. Someone else had put her name on the card, and she had no kids at home. I mentioned the fire, and she said it had burned her yard, a shed, and part of the other end of her house. She added, "Things have been really rough around here lately. I don't have insurance on the house, and I don't know what I'm going to do."

So I did what colporteurs do—I pulled out our books to offer her hope. After showing the little set, I said, "For a donation of any size, you can have some of these books. Would you like to look at them? Some people give some of their best pocket change for one of these books."

Kelsey's friend immediately reached into a pocket for money and held out a handful of change, saying, "Here, this is all I have." Kelsey chose *The Ministry of Healing* and *Bible Readings*.

Her friend went back inside, and we stood on the porch and talked for a moment. Then I said, "Let me pray with you before I go."

After the prayer she was wiping away tears. She said, "Please, can you wait here for a little bit?" She disappeared inside for several minutes; then she came out with a little ceramic cherub, playing a lyre, in her hand. "I want you to have this," she said, "and thank you so much for coming."

"I'll think of you and pray for you when I look at this little angel," I promised. I drove away, knowing I had been sent.

Miles away on another day, I was in another poor home, responding to a health lead. The clutter, filth, and squalor inside and out of the home were appalling. Again, I made my offer on our little set, but this man had no pocket change. I said, "We recycle cans for a special project. Would you like to give me a bag of cans for one of these books?" He took *The Ministry of Healing* and gathered up a bag of cans from around his porch. I smiled as I took the bag and handed him some *Our Little Friends* for his toddler also.

At another home Larry showed *The Bible Story* to a young father with three girls. His wife was at work at a laundromat, and he was out of work. He said he was registered with every temporary agency in town, but no jobs had come available. He seemed spiritually hungry but was completely out of money. So, while Larry packed up his briefcase, I asked, "Do you save your cans?" (I could see several empties in the room.) I made my offer about cans for books.

He said, "Really? Would you take cans for a book?"

I said, "Sure! Our job is to help people figure out ways so they can have some of these books."

He sent one of his kids out to gather some cans while he chose a book. He took *The Ministry of Healing*. She came back with a bag of strong-smelling beer cans—so I knew he had the right book! We also left some kids' magazines for the girls.

At a trailer in the country, we made one more spontaneous call. A young mother showed interest but said, "I don't get paid till Friday."

Larry said, "That's OK. Some people trade things for these books. We've even accepted Vidalia onions for them."

She replied, "Really? Those are Vidalias in that bag on the porch. You can take some."

Larry handed her the books and said, "You choose your book, and I'll choose my onions."

"I want this one," she said, taking *The Great Controversy*. "Just take the whole bag. People are always bringing me more onions at work. They grow them right down the road from there."

If we can just put the books into people's hands, it really doesn't matter how God pays us for our work—in money, little angels, empty beer cans, or even Vidalia onions. Praise the Lord!

Chapter 9

Not Forgotten

Craig's card was a request for *Great Stories for Kids*. The address was given as "Chaplan Rd." We studied our map and our GPS. Then Larry called 911 for clarification. They said it was a short lane going south off a road clearly marked on our map. It was definitely out in the sticks. We drove the full length of the country road, watching for Chapel Lane, but couldn't find it. We turned around and pulled off. I reached for my cell phone, knowing that the only way we might find Craig was to call his home directly before going.

    A woman answered and told me that Craig is her eleven-year-old son. She said to watch for a very sandy driveway on the left after several mailboxes. A mile or so later we found three mailboxes clumped together across from a very sandy lane. Some yellow scribbles on a rough board looked like it might say, "Chapel Lane." At the end of the drive were a couple of old, tin-roofed houses and a chicken pen.

    We stopped at the first one to ask for Craig. The house looked dirty inside without a lot of furniture. At least four very overweight adults lived there, and one woman was holding a baby. They directed us down a path just past the chicken pen. At the end of the path, we found a ragged-out, old, single-wide trailer surrounded by tall weeds and a lot of smashed soda cans littering the ground by the door. Sonya, a tired, middle-aged woman with graying hair met us at the door and invited us in.

    "Craig will be here in a minute," she said. "That's his handwriting. He goes to church but I just work."

    I glanced around the room. The kitchen cabinets had all been torn out and there was no stove or refrigerator. Closet doors on broken hinges sagged over some clutter where pantry doors should have been. The floor was made of worn OBS construction boards, full of splinters and covered with dust. At the far end of the room, a TV droned from its perch, high on a bookshelf, and a little desk held a small computer monitor. One recliner chair sat in front of the computer with a small side table full of magazines and household clutter. There was no other furniture.

I gasped, "It looks like someone took all your kitchen cabinets! How do you cook?"

"I don't," she replied. "This is the way I live."

"But what do you do for meals? How are you making it?" I asked.

"I eat one meal a day at work, and Craig takes his meals next door at my brother's house," she replied.

"Where do you work?" I asked. She said she worked in food service at a hospital. My mind had a hard time with their shattered lives, working all day with food, but no food at home—just sodas?!

When Craig came in, he hesitated to admit sending the card in. I pulled out our beautiful magabook series for children and a little sample of *The Bible Story* book. "Do you think you could give $5 or $10 for some of these?" I asked.

"I don't have any money unless you take change," Sonya said.

Across the room on the computer desk a few clear water bottles were lined up, full of organized change. I asked, "Would you like to give some change for one of these?"

They agreed and Sonya told Craig, "I'll get the wrappers. You count the nickels."

She handed him a bottle as he sat down in the recliner. I walked over and helped him wrap nickels while Sonya counted dimes.

"What grade are you in?" I asked.

"Fifth," he replied.

"Do you have any favorite subjects?"

"Math, science, and social studies," he said.

"Do you like to read?"

"Uh-huh."

> *I held out Real Heroes and Prince of Peace and asked, "Which one?" He looked at them for a moment and reached for Prince of Peace with the beautiful picture of Jesus riding on the donkey and all the people shouting hosannas. "That one," he said.*

"Then you'll enjoy these books," I said.

When Craig had counted five dollars in nickels, Sonya went on counting. "I'm going to get you that ten-dollar book too," she said. They handed me the rolled coins, and I held out *The Bible Story* and *Storybook*. Craig said softly to his mom, "But I wanted that other one."

I held out *Real Heroes* and *Prince of Peace* and asked, "Which one?"

He looked at them for a moment and reached for *Prince of Peace* with the beautiful picture of Jesus riding on the donkey and all the people shouting hosannas. "That one," he said.

"And we have something for Mom," I added.

Larry brought me my little bag, and I handed her *The Ministry of Healing* and an *Amazing Facts* Bible course card, inviting her to do it online. Sonya smiled her thanks. After a prayer for them, we said good-bye, thinking of their impoverished lives and how God made sure that Craig and his mother were not forgotten.

Chapter 10

A Dog, a Gun, a Prayer

The large, unlocked padlock hung to one side, so I drove through the open gate with a little prayer: "Please, Lord, don't let me get locked in here!" The driveway meandered along for another half mile before I came to the house. I picked up Gaylen's lead card, a sample *Foods* lead book, and my small book bags and started toward the door in the carport, but the big black collie began a terrible fuss. He was chained in the carport to guard the cars and the house, and he was doing a good job, barring my way to the door. I was glad he was chained.

I walked around to sliding glass doors at the other end and knocked. All was quiet. I knew if I didn't find Gaylen today, I might never find the gate open again. I couldn't call because his card gave no phone number. So, I wrote my name and phone number on the back of the card with a note and left it on the door with a little prayer, "This one's up to you. It's all I can do, Lord," and headed back to my car.

Just before I reached the car door, the house door in the carport opened, and a frowning man in jeans but no shirt, carrying a double-barreled shotgun stepped out and demanded, "What's going on out here? Nobody comes here without calling first!"

I smiled and held up the *Foods* book and asked, "Are you Gaylen? I'm sorry I couldn't call ahead. There wasn't any phone number on your card. You weren't home when I came by three months ago, and I was hoping to see you today. I left your card on the other door."

"Yes, I'm Gaylen," he said, quieting the dog.

"Do you remember looking at one of these books in a doctor's office?" I asked, holding out the book.

He put the gun down on his car and came to look at the book. "Yes, yes, I did look at one of these," he replied taking the book and paging through it. "I was in a doctor's office looking at the book. But I'm about to lose my job, and if the books are over $300, I can't order anything right now. No one wants to hire you if you're fifty-seven and have diabetes." He excused himself to go put a shirt on and came back and invited me in.

I handed him *Health Power* with a brief explanation, and he invited me to sit down while he looked through it. He said he would get that one because I had persisted in trying to find him. I sat on a heavy-duty coffee table while he sat across from me in his armchair. He pointed to the family pictures behind me and told me about his first family and how that marriage ended when his wife hit her midlife crisis in her mid-thirties. Later he was remarried to Wendy, a Filipino nurse, and they have a ten-year-old, Haley, who is the joy of their lives.

A thick paperback book sat on the table beside me—*Thirty-seven Amazing Bible Prophecies You Need to Know*, so I was sure Gaylen was into Bible things. He went upstairs for the money for *Health Power* while I waited. When he came back, I mentioned his book and said I always like to leave a gift book with people and I thought he would like this one—*The Great Controversy Ended*.

He took the book and started talking about the Bible and his perception of end times and prophecies he had studied. Suddenly we were friends anticipating the coming of Jesus together. As he talked about prophecies, I told him I was sure he would enjoy the book because it addresses all these issues. I asked if I could have a prayer for his family before I left, and he came across the room for prayer. When I finished my prayer, Gaylen prayed an earnest prayer for us as well. It was a real transformation visit from a dog and a gun to a prayer!

Chapter 11

Poking Holes in the Dark

I prayed, "Lord, whom do you want me to see next?" It would be dark in less than an hour and the next lead was thirty miles away. Turning at the next corner, I decided, "Why not here?" It looked like most of the people were home, so I reached for my clipboard.

At the first house a large man with a fat wad of tobacco in his cheek stepped out and did the survey. In the middle of our conversation, he took a call from his pharmacist about his blood pressure medication. I left him with some literature and a stop smoking pamphlet. Around the corner a mother gave five dollars *for The Desire of Ages* for her seventeen-year-old daughter and signed up for the *Amazing Facts* Bible course.

At the next house a young dad became interested. They couldn't do big books, but he said, "I have five dollars." He really wanted *The Great Controversy*. He called his wife to the door and asked me, "Would you tell her what you just told me about these books?"

I explained the little books again and handed them to her to look through, and she invited me in. We stepped into a very clean living room where two little blond-headed boys were playing. The man came back, smoothing out his five-dollar bill.

The wife explained, "We're trying to settle on a church to go to."

He was raised in one church, and she was raised in another, but they wanted the family to be together in church. "We've about settled on Southern Baptist," she concluded.

I said, "These books will give you Bible answers."

He said, "I wish we could get them all."

They chose *The Great Controversy*, and I handed them a *Bible Readings* also and said, "These will really help you solve your differences." I left some *Our Little Friends* and *Keys to Happiness* and signed them up for the Bible course. Next door, I remembered that I wanted to give the young couple a stop smoking tract, so I walked back, saying, "I just wanted you to have this bookmark. Maybe it's for your husband." They were already sitting down to read their new books. She took it with a smile and said, "Yes, that's our dirtiest habit!"

The next mom was interested but out of money. She took *Keys to Happiness* and signed up for the Bible course. Her four girls crowded around to get *Primary Treasures*. At the next place I spoke with a man beside his pickup truck full of painting supplies. He said, "My mom had these when I was a kid. I was raised Methodist, changed to Baptist, and now I'm married to a Catholic." He took the *Christ's Object Lessons*.

The mother at the next home had three children. She was a career homemaker and the place was clean and cheery. She said she really wished she could get all the books right now, but she explained, "My father is dying and I have to pay for his funeral. His insurance already told me that his coverage is inadequate, so I'm saving all I can to deal with it."

She took the *Keys to Happiness* and said, "Oh, what a pretty book! I just love birds, and we have all kinds of pets for the kids." She signed up for the Bible course and took some *Primary Treasures* and *Our Little Friends* for the children.

Dusk was falling as I stopped at the last home. The couple was smoking, sitting on their steps with their poodle and Chihuahua. They paused for the survey and looked at the little books. They wouldn't be paid until Friday but they accepted *Keys to Happiness*, a stop smoking tract, and signed up for *Amazing Facts*. I drove away satisfied. I had the joy of poking some more holes in the dark.

CHAPTER 12

Sudden Opportunity

He was tall, strong, and cheerful. He made some friendly comments as he helped us carry our new equipment out to our camper. As we were thanking him, I turned to get a gift book for him from our vehicle.

I asked, "Do you like to read?"

"Oh, yes! I read all the time," he answered.

"Do you like to read history?" I asked.

"I love it!" he replied and told me about a book he was just finishing.

I pulled out a copy of *The Great Controversy* and said, "Then you should enjoy this one. It tells the history of Christianity and expands on Revelation. It goes into the Dark Ages and brings it on up to our day and the future."

"Oh, thank you! I'll read it," he said reaching eagerly for the book and putting his other hand into his pocket for some money. He asked, "How much do I owe you for it?"

"Oh, that's our gift to you just for helping us carry our stuff," I smiled. "But if you'd like to give twenty dollars, you can have the rest of the set. There are five more."

I reached for the other books and began naming them off with a one-sentence description of each book.

When I got to the third book, *The Ministry of Healing*, he said, "You don't have to sell me on these. I'll take them!" He handed me the twenty dollars and took the set. We got in and fastened our seat belts, and Larry burst out laughing. I laughed with him and exclaimed, "Praise the Lord! It was a sudden opportunity. I might never see that man again!"

Chapter 13

For Melissa

I couldn't find my lead, so I started knocking to see a few more people before dark. Melissa opened her door asked, "Who are you and where are you from?"

I held out a flyer and said, "I'm with *The Bible Story*, those blue books you see in the doctor's office. Have you seen those before?"

"Oh, yes," she said. "Would you like to come in and get out of this heat?"

We sat down at her kitchen table and she asked, "Haven't we met somewhere before? You just look so familiar!"

She said she had the books years ago. "But my brother has them for his kids now, and I know I'll get them back for my grandchildren later," she finished.

"Let me show you something really nice that we have," I said pulling out some of our magabooks—*My Friend Jesus, Storybook, Peace Above the Storm, God's Answers, Foods That Heal*. As Melissa glanced through *Foods That Heal*, she said, "This is good. I'm a nurse, so I'm familiar with some of this."

She told me where she worked, and I said, "Oh, I've been going in there for the last twelve years to check *The Bible Story* book!"

Melissa laughed, "That's where I've seen you before. That's why you look familiar!"

When I asked if she would like to give a donation for some of the books, she gave a strong, "Yes!" and went to get her checkbook.

Then she asked, "Do you have a few minutes? May I share something with you?" She left the kitchen and came back clutching something to her heart. "I share this story whenever I can," she began.

About three years before, her husband and son-in-law were drowned in a tragic boating accident. In fact, the son-in-law was lost under the water for ten days. They buried her husband, not knowing if they would ever find the son-in-law. A year later she just wanted to get away for a while. So, she took her two grown daughters and their little children to their timeshare vacation spot in another country.

On the very day of the anniversary of her loss, she told me she was walking the beach alone, drawing hearts in the sand and "bawling her heart out" to God, grieving her dear husband of thirty years. Suddenly, a wave swept up something at her feet. She reached down to grasp it quickly. It was a piece of shell or worn coral, smoothed by waves and sand into a beautiful little heart. She stared at it in her hand, praising God through her tears that He had remembered her.

"And here it is," she finished as she handed me the frame. There was the little heart, mounted behind glass. She told me, "I don't understand God's will, but I believe He has used me through it all."

She started a widows' support group. As she waited for the ladies to come for the first meeting, she could see her own shadow on the wall, and she thought, "How can this be? How can I be a widow? I was supposed to retire in a few years and just enjoy life together with him."

Then she said, "Other people have told me that they have taken courage in difficulties because they say, 'If Melissa can hold up under what she's been through, we can too.'"

I read to her from *Peace Above the Storm*, where it says: "No tears are shed that God does not notice. There is no smile that He does not mark."[3]

When I looked up, she said, "I can't wait to start reading!" We prayed together, and I knew I had been sent down that road, not for a mobile home park, but for Melissa.

---

3 Ellen G. White, *Peace Above the Storm* (Nampa, ID: Pacific Press, 1994), p. 76.

Chapter 14

Why Am I Knocking *Here*?

It was a hot July morning. People were sitting on a bench swing or standing around smoking in the sketchy shade of a deformed oak tree when I pulled into the bare dirt yard. Someone went into the house to get Trina for me. I held out two of *The Bible Story* cards and asked, "Did you send these in?"

"Yes," she replied. "We look at those at the doctor's office."

As we talked, I learned that Trina was not working at the time, but she was hopeful that her next interview at the Department of Labor would yield a job. Several of her relatives lived at this house, surviving on minimal income. I offered Trina our small paperbacks for a donation, but she could do nothing today, so I left her with a prayer, a Bible course enrollment card, and a *Happiness Digest*.

I drove on to find my next lead on Graham Street. But the numbers on Graham Street did not match my card at all. I looked closer at the card. It read: "A. F. Graham Road," a location out in the country. I chided myself for reading it incorrectly and pulled into some shade to study the map. Then I remembered my plan for the day: 1) Run inner city leads in the morning then knock spontaneously until lunch. 2) Advertise after lunch. 3) Run country leads.

"I'll stick to the plan and start here," I said aloud. I grabbed my clipboard and book bags and walked back to the closest house, a small, messy-looking place with a damaged screen door. "Why am I knocking *here*?" I questioned myself.

An older man invited me in, and we sat in his cluttered, roach-infested living room and went through my five questions. When I handed him *The Bible Story* flyer, he talked with me about his own spiritual concerns. I showed him our small softbacks, and he said, "Well, I don't have any children, but if you go down to the end of the block, a woman there would be really interested in these."

"Which house?" I asked.

"Actually, it's around the corner and just before the big road," he replied. "Her name is Trina and her two kids are like grandchildren to me. I used to work with her dad and we were really good friends. Then when I got sick and spent six months in the hospital, he came every day to see me."

"I know who you are talking about," I replied. "I met Trina just a little while ago. She sent a card in for these books."

"Did she get them?" Carver asked.

"No, she didn't have any money today," I answered.

Carver whipped out his cell phone and began punching in numbers. "Is Trina there? Let me talk to Trina," he demanded. "That woman is here with those Bible books. Do you want these books? Do you want them? I'll get them and you send Billy down here to pick them up. Let me talk to your dad."

I watched in amazement. Here was a man, barely surviving in a hovel, not willing to get books for himself, but moved by love to invest in someone else. Carver stayed on the phone for several minutes, then reached for the little books and carefully counted out his money. After a prayer together, I walked back out into the sweltering heat, in awe of God answering my question, "Why am I knocking *here*?"

Chapter 15

Mystery Lead Cards

"Yes, I'm Krista, but I didn't send that in," she said as she took *The Bible Story* lead card from Larry's hand. "That's not my handwriting!"

Krista was sitting with friends around her dining room table, visiting and receiving customers for candy bars through her back door. A shelf loaded with brightly colored candies and snacks stretched along the wall. A handicapped daughter sat in a wheelchair at the other end of the table. The ladies gathered around to see the card and identify the handwriting.

"That's Bob's handwriting, but he doesn't live here anymore," they agreed.

Krista didn't want to look at the big books, so Larry asked if she liked to read the Bible. She said yes, so we pulled out some magabooks. Krista was impressed but said she didn't have much money. She reached for the *God's Answers* and thumbed through it.

"This is really good," she mused. "I'd like to have this and that other one, *The Great Controversy*, but I can only give ten dollars."

I glanced at the books. The *God's Answers* was showing some wear on the cover, so I asked, "Would you like to give ten dollars for these two books?"

"Yes," she replied, reaching for her candy money and counting out ten one-dollar bills.

I held some books toward another lady and asked, "Would you like to look at these?"

She nodded and asked, "Do you have any more of those question-and-answer books?"

I said, "I'm sorry, that was my last one just like that, but I have a little pocket edition out in the car. I'll go get it for you." So, she took *Bible Readings* and *Jesus Friend of Children*.

Then Larry asked Krista if she would like a money saver. She said yes, so he handed her the little *Vibrant Life* tract on how to quit smoking. She looked at the cover and laughed, "Oh, yes, I've been wanting to quit and everyone is after me about it!" One or two of the other ladies reached out for their copy so they could quit, too, and they were all sincerely glad for Larry to pray for God to help them before we left.

We ran the next mystery card with similar handwriting, and Amy met us at the door. She said, "No, I didn't send that. That's not my handwriting. Maybe that's my son's handwriting, but he's not here. He's thirty-four years old."

We started to show her magabooks at the door and she invited us in. She said, "I've really been going through a lot lately. I've hit menopause and my health is messed up, and my husband just got out of prison after being in for eleven years. So, he's trying to adjust, and there's just a lot going on around here." There Amy stood in her beautiful house, surrounded by beautiful things, explaining that she had hardly any money and she felt like she was falling apart.

She said some Mormon boys had come by earlier, but she just didn't want to talk with them, so they offered a prayer for her, and she had felt better. She wondered how that was possible. Larry said, "It's been scientifically proven that people who are prayed for get better."

I showed her *The Ministry of Healing* and read about God's love and care and Amy said, "I've only got seven dollars, but I've got to have that book!" She went and got her five-dollar bill.

Then Larry said, "And you need a prayer before we leave."

She grasped our hands and Larry prayed. When we looked up, she had tears in her eyes, so I offered, "Do you need a hug?"

Amy threw her arms around me and buried her face on my shoulder. She began crying aloud, and I could feel the tears pouring onto my shoulder. I just held Amy for a long moment until the sobbing ended; then I told her God would help her through this. We were sure it was for her we had received that mystery card.

Chapter 16

A Call to Prayer

In most of the United States, the territory is wide open for mission-minded workers. Over and over, we meet people who have sent in cards who are wondering if they will ever get an answer. Please join us in praying that God will raise up canvassers for His work.

Many think they are unable, but God doesn't call the able, He enables the called. I think of our work when I read these two sentences from *The Acts of the Apostles*: *"Day by day God works with him, perfecting the character that is to stand in the time of final test. And day by day the believer is working out before men and angels a sublime experiment, showing what the gospel can do for fallen human beings."*[4]

Could God be calling you to become a sublime experiment in literature evangelism?

For more information on how to support or become more involved in literature evangelism, contact the publishing department of your local conference of Seventh-day Adventists.

---

4 Ellen G. White, *The Acts of the Apostles* (Mountain View, CA: Pacific Press, 1911), p. 585, emphasis mine.

Part III

A SIMPLE TOOL
The Character-Building Survey

Chapter 1

Using the Character-Building Survey

Here are a few points on how we use the character-building survey to see more people. Each survey page has many blanks per question so we can go to many houses before shuffling papers to a fresh page. We keep two or three copies of the survey on our clipboard, and behind the survey sheets we have a few of *The Bible Story* cards or brochures.

At the door we get into the survey as soon as possible (without wasting time telling them our names and where we are from—we get into that later if they are interested in what we are doing). We know we need to get their interest in that first thirty seconds or we may not get it at all.

We say basically: "Hello. How are you? We're visiting some of the folks in the area with a short questionnaire on character building. Just five short questions, OK?"

At their consent, I start right in with the first question: "On a scale of one to ten, ten being highest and one being lowest, how important do you feel religious training is for children?" Most people have a strong opinion on this and say, "Ten!" If they say, "Really important," I respond, "So you'd give that a ten?"

Then I go right on to number two: "Where is the most important place for children to learn about the Bible?" We mostly get two different answers on this one: "Church" or "Home."

Then I say, "The last three questions are just Yes or No." Then I go on with the questions. I try not to get into much discussion as I go through the questions because I told them they are brief questions.

At the end I say something like, "Thank you for your participation," or "That was easy, wasn't it?" Then I go on to tell who we are with and what we are offering: "We're with *The Bible Story* company. You may be familiar with some of our materials," as I hand them one of the flyers from behind the survey sheets. "You may have seen some of these around in your doctor's office or different places. We're trying to help families in teaching children the important things like respect, obedience, honesty, and kindness through the stories of the Bible. If you felt that *The Bible Story* or some of our other materials could help your children to have a good attitude and stay out of trouble, would you like to take a few minutes and look at some of this today?"

At this point some will say yes and invite us in, but most people will give an objection or an excuse why they can't take time right now. For these people, I immediately reach into my shoulder bag and start canvassing them on the spot. If children are obviously part of the home, I reach for children's magabooks. If there are no kids, I ask, "Do you like to read and study the Bible yourself?" and pull out all five little books so they can see them all at once.

I tell them just a bit about each book, and then I say, "We offer these on a donation basis. The suggested donation is $5 each or $20 for the set, some people give more, some less. Would you like to give something for some of these today?" Many people will give at least $5 for one book, and a lot of people take the $20 offer. If they hesitate over money, I urge, "For a donation of any size, you can have one of these books." (They need the books!) We have even traded for a variety of things, mostly food stuff.

Then we always try to leave something free—at least a *Happiness Digest*, a tract, or a Bible lesson. This method has upped our demos and orders by at least 35 percent. Why not try it?

Chapter 2

Spontaneous Survey Responses

How can an LE see more people? One way is using the simple, five-question survey on character building. It has been interesting, but people who give the "right" answers are not necessarily going to get books today. Here are our results from 5,607 surveys over three-and-a-half years.

1. On a scale of 1 to 10, (10 being the highest and 1 being the lowest) how important do you feel religious training is for children?

Highest: 10	Range: 6 to 9	Range: 5 or less
87%	11%	2%

2. Where is the most important place for children to learn about the Bible?

Church or Sunday school	Home
50%	49%

3. Do you think that children are learning enough about the Bible at school?

No	Yes	Other
88%	7%	5%

4. **Do you think that they are learning enough about the Bible from TV or the media?**

No	Yes	Some
87%	8%	3%

5. **Do you think that children are learning enough about the Bible from their friends?**

No	Yes	Some
79%	10%	7%

So, what difference does it make? Several factors make an impact on our work:

1) We have left some form of literature in 5,600 homes that we wouldn't have if we hadn't knocked.

2) Often people warm up and become friendly as we do the survey. They are more receptive to whatever we have to offer.

3) We have had 20 to 30 percent more in orders than we would have if we only ran leads and didn't knock on doors.

4) We have had hundreds more people accept the Bible lesson enrollment cards than if we hadn't knocked.

5) We have placed hundreds of little books on a donation basis during this time. Cash flow for small books has increased from an average of about $200 a month to over $500 a month when we consistently see people. Some outstanding months have brought in over $900 in small books or magabooks.

6) We have made better use of our time by seeing more people in a given area and we have met a much greater cross section of humanity and its woes.

7) If we don't go see the people, who will?

No tools will work in this ministry without prayer. That is a given. There are many tools to do this work. The survey is just one of them, but it works when we work it.

(A copy of the survey is on the next page. Feel free to run copies and adapt it to your own personal evangelism work.)

Chapter 3

LE Character-Building Survey

1. On a scale of 1 to 10, (10 being the highest and 1 being the lowest) how important do you feel religious training is for children?

   1._____ 5._____ 9._____ 13._____ 17._____

   2._____ 6._____ 10._____ 14._____ 18._____

   3._____ 7._____ 11._____ 15._____ 19._____

   4._____ 8._____ 12._____ 16._____ 20._____

2. Where is the most important place for children to learn about the Bible?

   1._____ 5._____ 9._____ 13._____ 17._____

   2._____ 6._____ 10._____ 14._____ 18._____

   3._____ 7._____ 11._____ 15._____ 19._____

   4._____ 8._____ 12._____ 16._____ 20._____

3. **Do you think that children are learning enough about the Bible at school?**

1._____ 5._____ 9._____ 13._____ 17._____

2._____ 6._____ 10._____ 14._____ 18._____

3._____ 7._____ 11._____ 15._____ 19._____

4._____ 8._____ 12._____ 16._____ 20._____

4. **Do you think that they are learning enough about the Bible from TV or the media?**

1._____ 5._____ 9._____ 13._____ 17._____

2._____ 6._____ 10._____ 14._____ 18._____

3._____ 7._____ 11._____ 15._____ 19._____

4._____ 8._____ 12._____ 16._____ 20._____

5. **Do you think that children are learning enough about the Bible from their friends?**

1._____ 5._____ 9._____ 13._____ 17._____

2._____ 6._____ 10._____ 14._____ 18._____

3._____ 7._____ 11._____ 15._____ 19._____

4._____ 8._____ 12._____ 16._____ 20._____

Bibliography

White, Ellen G. *The Desire of Ages.* Mountain View, CA: Pacific Press Publishing Association, 1898.

White, Ellen G. *Colporteur Ministry.* Mountain View, CA: Pacific Press Publishing Association, 1953.

White, Ellen G. *Peace Above the Storm.* Nampa, ID: Pacific Press Publishing Association, 1994.

White, Ellen G. *The Acts of the Apostles.* Mountain View, CA: Pacific Press Publishing Association, 1911.

TEACH Services, Inc.
P U B L I S H I N G

We invite you to view the complete
selection of titles we publish at:
www.TEACHServices.com

We encourage you to write us
with your thoughts about this,
or any other book we publish at:
info@TEACHServices.com

TEACH Services' titles may be purchased in
bulk quantities for educational, fund-raising,
business, or promotional use.
bulksales@TEACHServices.com

Finally, if you are interested in seeing
your own book in print, please contact us at:
publishing@TEACHServices.com
We are happy to review your manuscript at no charge.

www.ingramcontent.com/pod-product-compliance
Lightning Source LLC
Chambersburg PA
CBHW070542170426
43200CB00011B/2517